C000047339

This book is dedicated to Ewelina Dymek,
the illustrator of *This Year Will Be Different*,
who's responsible for at least half of the
success of my first year as a freelancer.

This project wouldn't have been possible
without the great help of Diana Ovezea,
Sara Combs, and Diana Joiner, who have
put all their energy into creating this
book you're now holding in your hands!

© 2016, Monika Kanokova | www.mkaystudio.com

Editor:	**Monika Kanokova**
	hello@mkanokova.com
Copy Editor:	**Diana J. Joiner**
	djjoiner925@gmail.com
Illustrator:	**Sara Combs**
	sara@designcomb.com
Art Director:	**Diana Ovezea**
	type.design@me.com

The moral rights of the authors have been asserted.

Should you be holding a copy of this book you did not pay for, be an awesome human and do a good deed today to serve your local community, or make the first person you meet today smile from ear to ear.

A CIP catalogue record for this book is available from the National Library in Austria.

Proudly self-published in Austria in 2016.
ISBN: 978-3-9503967-9-9

Monika Kanokova

MY CREATIVE ~~SIDE~~ BUSINESS

#SMARTCREATIVES

The fascinating stories of 14 women
who rock their creative businesses

CONTENTS

Hello there!

Let me guess, you picked up (or downloaded) this book because you're curious. Perhaps more specifically, you're curious to know what it means to run a business while maintaining your creative freedom. Maybe you're looking to establish a side hustle, or maybe you already are a freelancer, but are wondering how to stabilize your business. Regardless of where you stand on the spectrum, this book just might answer all of your questions!

When I first went freelance, I wondered how I could set up a business and earn enough money to support myself from day one. I didn't have any savings, so having a functioning freelance career was crucial. Writing my first book, *This Year Will Be Different: The Insightful Guide to Becoming a Freelancer,* helped me find my way. It also helped me reach my current checkpoint: wondering how to take the next step to transition from solely being a freelancer to running a creative business.

If you would like to know how to earn money, even while you go on vacation or are sick in bed, then this book was written for you. Don't get me wrong, this isn't about getting money without doing anything to have earned it. This book is to help you understand some principles and strategies to not just work harder, but to work *smarter*. It's meant to give you context to what it really means to do creative work and build a business that's not based on a quick payout. Here, you'll find honest stories of people who work hard on what they truly enjoy; people who pursue long-term goals and strive for a life that grants them creative freedom. There are different ways to grow a creative business. You can either hire people and go from being a solopreneur to being an employer, you can find partners to distribute and sell your creative work for you, or you can build a following and capitalize on the number of people interested in hearing from you regularly. For this book, I interviewed 14 inspiring women from around the world to better understand how they built multiple income streams. The result, and what you're about to dive into, is a guide focused on building a stable solopreneur business by helping you grasp more about establishing distribution partnerships, licensing and royalties, capitalizing on your online following, and much, much more.

Many of the women I talked to are multi-passionate and proud to have found different creative outlets that help them make a living as creatives. For once, it's not a book that advises you to focus on one thing and one thing only, but instead, inspires you to make the most out of your creativity and your personal style. What I believe distinguishes these women is that they've invested their time to be fully dedicated to building businesses they would want to work for themselves. They also don't slave away and undersell their services. Whenever they don't have clients, they think of a project that excites them and work on that instead.

If you've read my first book, *This Year Will Be Different,* you may remember Oren Lasry's advice that you can't just work *in* your business, but that you must also work *on* your business. That's what I'm inviting you to do, and the knowledge shared in this book will help you do exactly that! Grab a pen or a highlighter and scribble notes as you read! My secret ambition (but I suppose not so secret anymore) was to write a book that the reader (you) would want to highlight from the beginning to the end. I hope that you'll find value, not just in the words written especially for you, but also in between the lines where you'll realize your own strengths and verbalize your own interests. I hope you gain as much from reading *My Creative (Side) Business* as I have from writing it.

I'll tell you now (and will tell you again at the end) to get in touch if you have any questions or additional ideas. Also, I'd love for you to share your learnings and what this book has inspired you to do on social media, so we can follow up with your future endeavors.

Use the hashtag #SMARTCREATIVES so we, and other readers, can see your creative business grow! We're all in this together, and I hope we all make it!

Thank you once again for picking up this book. Now, let's turn your passions into multiple side businesses!

Love,
Monika

START WITH A SIDE PROJECT

When you think about why you admire the people you do, it's mostly because they have some sort of a project that you stumbled upon and loved. No matter if it's a big or small project, it's something that's significant enough for you to notice and associate with. Now, it's your turn to have that effect on someone else.

It doesn't matter whether you're a freelancer and you offer your services to others, or if you work for someone else and are dreaming of freelancing; the secret to a fulfilling career is taking the effort to make something happen that you want to be known for.

Choose whatever you want to reach next and start working on it, be it a book, a graphic novel, a series of paintings, or an app that you've always wanted to develop. It could even be a fashion collection; it really doesn't matter! Part of working on your business is doing something that allows you to have full creative control. This isn't about money because you'll probably spend more than you'll earn from this project. This is about investing in yourself, your career, and your reputation. This side project is here to have something to talk about, to give people an anchor for them to associate something specific with you. Your side project is your most accurate business card.

Having a side project doesn't just come in handy if you don't have any references to start out as a freelancer. A side project is there to give people a clear sign to where you want to go next.

When you think about it, every time someone sees your CV, they learn all about your past, but a side project helps showcase where you're heading. Your side project is your entrance ticket to wherever you want to go in the future. It's the most crucial building block of your creative business, and it's the first thing you should mention whenever someone asks you what you do to grow your business.

Given how much I built up the importance of a side project, you might feel a bit intimidated if you don't have something specific you want to work on. *Breathe.*

As big as a side project sounds, it can be simplified so that anyone can start working on one, even as soon as tomorrow. A project is always something that has a specific duration and a clear accountable goal. A good timeframe for you to start with might be a month.

The next question is what will you work on? The answer to this is simple: work on whatever you want to be hired for. If you want people to pay you for writing fiction, then you have 30 days of writing fiction ahead of you. If you want people to hire you for illustrations, you have 30 days of illustrating ahead of you. You get the point. You need to work on something you want others to associate with you, so it's entirely up to you and your interests.

Next, we need to make your project more specific. You'll need to pick a theme, a very specific topic that you'll explore from different angles. You can draw a cat every day or write a 200-word story about a person you saw on the subway. Whatever it is, try to make your project figurative and accountable in one way or another. Whether you give yourself a timeframe every day, like drawing for 20 minutes or writing a short story with a specific length, try to find a way to make it easy for you to feel like you've accomplished something.

Once you have an activity, a theme, and a timeframe, it's time to make yourself follow through. Having a plan is one thing, but following through is a completely different story. Personally, I'm a huge fan of social pressure. Once you share your plans with people around you, you're far more likely to do whatever you said you would. Having a public deadline and letting people follow along will not only help you commit, but it will also inspire them to follow your lead. Social media is a wonderful tool to create out loud and let others participate in your process. You can be open about wanting to learn a new technique and let people see how your skills evolve. Nothing is quite as inspiring as seeing the struggle others

GIVE YOURSELF
THE FREEDOM TO
EXPERIMENT.

have gone through to reach where they are now. (Whenever you struggle, watch Karen Cheng's TEDx talk.) Once you commit and talk about your side project throughout your journey, you've created an authentic way to talk about your business.

If you're someone who needs social pressure to get things done, then you can also participate in collective creative projects. National Novel Writing Month, better known as #NaNoWriMo in November, is a collective attempt to write a first draft of a 50,000-word novel. #The100DayProject is a creative hashtag project that prompts people to doing something creative for 100 straight days. There are several communities out there, and not to forget, you can also pull together your own local community to work on side projects alongside others. It's like book clubs. But different.

IT'S TIME FOR YOU TO START NOW!

Throughout the years that I've been talking to people about their careers, I've often heard that many of them started as a side project. Many professional bloggers never intended to make money, many makers started out with a small Etsy store, and many people who pivoted their businesses to transition into new creative careers did so because they had a side project they were truly passionate about. It all really does begin with a project!

When I talked to Sara, she told me how she began her illustration business with #The100DayProject where she created patterns inspired by San Francisco for a hundred consecutive days. Not only has she since received requests to commission her artwork, but she now gets hired to illustrate too. After the interview, I was so inspired by her story and I loved her artwork so much that I hired her to illustrate the series of learnings in this book. (Thank you, dear.) For Sara and many others, it all started with a simple 100-day side project. I'm curious to see what could inspire you to create something special and where it can lead you in the future! Aren't you?

Sara Combs

Sara is a UI/UX designer and a passionate Airbnb host. When she began her #The100DayProject, she didn't know she would soon receive requests to license her artwork.

In her interview, Sara talks about the importance of having a hobby that you should post on social media and how she found great mentors for her work.

📍 **San Francisco, USA**

1. What's your educational background and how did you arrive to where you are now?

I studied environmental design at the Maryland Institute College of Art because I've always been interested in experimenting with space and objects and how our surroundings influence us. After graduation, I created my own jewelry line before taking on a full-time job as a UI/UX designer. After over two years, my husband, who was also my colleague, and I found ourselves increasingly unhappy with our jobs. We craved more flexibility, as well as the energy to devote ourselves to our own projects. After a wonderful weekend away in wine country (and perhaps some day drinking), we left feeling ready to make a change and start our own design studio. At that point, I made the conscious decision to leave my job rather than wait. It felt too easy to make excuses about leaving with the holidays and another vacation approaching. I knew that if I didn't act soon, I might not end up going through with it.

We'd already been doing some freelancing on the side, which definitely helped ease us into full-time contract work. We were also lucky to have a great support system from previous co-workers who would send work our way. Once we got our first clients, we found that our business began to grow by word-of-mouth. After offering our best work, clients were happy to refer us to other companies who they'd heard needed design help as well. That's how we managed to grow our design studio fairly quickly.

2. What are your different income streams?

My husband and I have had our design studio since the end of 2013. We work with startups and mid-sized companies. I'm licensing illustrations and patterns to various companies, and we also have a house, The Joshua Tree House, on Airbnb.

3. Why and how did you launch your different income streams?

In 2013, my husband and I left our full-time jobs as UI/UX designers and decided to start our own business. We wanted the flexibility to work on a variety of projects that truly excited us and the freedom to get creative with non-traditional income streams.

Running our own design studio has given us the opportunity to run our businesses the way we want. It also allows us to push boundaries and see what kind of working lifestyle we can get away with. In 2014, we spent five months living in New York and then two months traveling Southeast Asia while working for our clients. Being in Asia and exploring the world from a different angle was amazing, but also challenging because it's not always easy to find functioning internet and be there for your clients when they need to get in touch quickly. We worked less while we were there, but also spent less, so we returned home with a little extra cash than if we had just stayed in San Francisco and continued working nonstop.

After a year of working on projects for our design studio, we found that success meant we were working longer and longer hours. We realized this wasn't sustainable. We didn't want to find ourselves burnt out and defeated in five years, ready to go back to full-time jobs just to have our weekends back. At that point, we decided rather than grow our team, we would focus on establishing multiple, passive income streams. I started licensing some of my artwork for stationery and fabric lines, and also created our first Airbnb business. Our aim was to find ways to make money while taking on less client-related projects. We wanted to make time for more personal projects and have the freedom to travel more often. It's your decision how you want your business to be.

Because we spent so much time traveling and gathering inspiration in 2014, when we got back home, I decided to make 2015 the year of creating. When I heard Elle Luna speak about #The100DayProject, a project that encourages you to share your process of creativity on social media for 100 days, I was immediately intrigued. Being a part of a bigger community was exactly what I needed to create every day, and because I was craving working with my hands, I decided to paint patterns that were inspired by San Francisco. Because you had to share your work on Instagram each day, I shared everything I created; the work I liked and the work I didn't like as much. It's scary sharing work that doesn't feel perfect or finished. Social media is really incredible if you're able to let down your barriers and share your work and thoughts openly.

It was surprising for me to see that people really resonated with my creations. A lot of people reposted and repinned my patterns and one day, someone reached out to me and asked if I was interested in licensing my patterns to them. I didn't know anything about licensing, so I talked to a good friend of mine and used Google as a resource as well.

"SHARE YOUR PROCESS OF CREATIVITY."

There are multiple ways to license: if it's for a one-time use, you can ask for a one-off fee. If your artwork will be on T-shirts or something that's being reproduced and sold, you can ask for a flat-fee and royalties. It's normal to receive anything between 3–15% of the retail price. The percentage varies depending on the scale of the company you're working with and their quantity of sales. Smaller companies will offer higher royalties, while larger companies will offer smaller percentages.

Now that #The100DayProject is over, my patterns are for sale as iPhone cases on Casetify, stationery at PunkPost, and as a fabric line at Guildery. I have a licensing contract with everyone I work with where I also make sure I state the timeframe of the licensing agreement. You can either license your patterns exclusively to a brand or non-exclusively, and then you can reuse the same design several times. It's important to set rates you feel comfortable with.

Then, we have our Airbnb house. We love creating experiences and figured having a home that was meant for people to reset, reflect, and create in would be an incredible project. We also realized that it had good income opportunities with a lot of visitors to the area and affordable real estate. We were looking at different houses and the one we decided to go for was a house for sale by the owner we found on Craigslist. It was a bit scary that we didn't go through a real estate agent the first time we bought a house, but it all worked out. The house has already been profitable, but the best thing about it is you get to communicate with so many different people, which I love. Many visitors told us they'd been following the Instagram account of @thejoshuatreehouse and really wanted to spend time there.

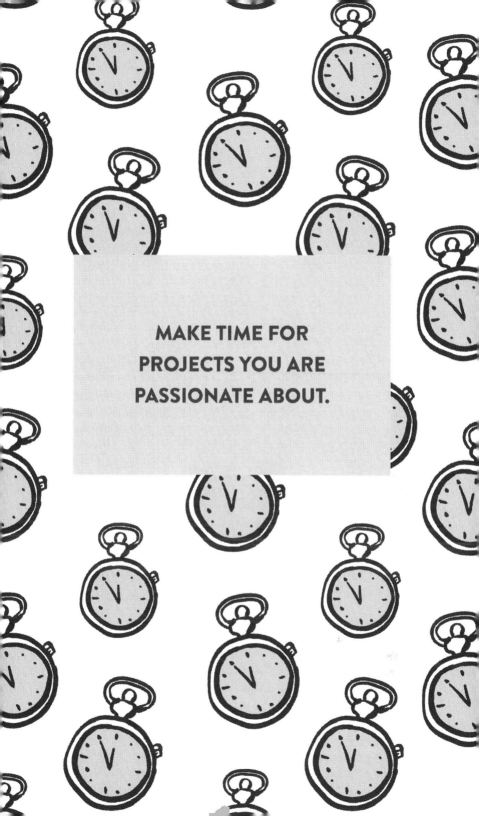

MAKE TIME FOR PROJECTS YOU ARE PASSIONATE ABOUT.

We did all the renovation work ourselves to reduce the spendings. We spent most of the summer in Joshua Tree and painted, renovated, and furnished everything. As a designer, and in order to be able to do something like that, you need retainer clients. You can't go out looking for clients all the time if you want to play around with exploring new possibilities, such as the Airbnb or my creative work. To turn our clients to retainer clients, we thought about who needed more regular work from us and then approached them with a suggestion of how many hours a month we could spend working on their projects. For this consistent work, we created monthly budgets with our clients rather than working hourly or by project fee. Some of our clients needed that sort of service and some didn't, so we approached the ones who did!

4. How do you structure your days?

Usually, the first thing I do in the morning is share something on our @joshuatreehouse Instagram account. Social media helps us tell a story about our house, which brings it to life and gives it more purpose than just being a vacation rental. It's been a wonderful experience so far and it has us craving opening up more Airbnbs in the future. We either share photos that we took ourselves or photos that our guests have hashtagged. After I've checked that everything is going smoothly with our Airbnb, I jump into doing client work. I like to work either from home or at a coffee shop to switch it up and get a change of scenery. In the afternoon, I try to focus on my personal work if there isn't anything else that's urgent.

The biggest learning for me last year was that you don't need anyone to hire you for something. If you want to do something, you should just do it! You can probably make money off of it later, which didn't occur to me until people started approaching me on Instagram to license my patterns.

**"YOU DON'T NEED ANYONE
TO HIRE YOU TO DO SOMETHING.
JUST START CREATING!"**

When you first start out, it's good to have restrictions on your design work. For me, #The100DayProject did just that, so it's been a bit harder to keep creating and sharing my work online without such a framework. I've been trying to set time aside to do work that's for me. Whenever possible, I set aside some time in the afternoon to paint. I've been trying to force myself to share some recent work, but it's much harder if you don't have the positive pressure to post that comes with being a part of #The100DayProject.

The more money we can manage to earn with our commodities, the more pressure is taken off of our client work, which allows us to focus. My aim is to create a lifestyle brand and focus on creating home goods and fabric lines. Our Airbnb is already the equivalent in earnings to one large project each year.

5. What do you do yourself and what do you outsource?

I believe that you should do the things yourself that you do best, so in my case, that's design work, and then outsource everything that you're not as good at. Accounting and cleaning our Airbnb is outsourced. We also have a key box, so apart from the communication with our cleaner and the guests, there's not much left to do.

With licensing, if you have strong partners, you can outsource all of the logistics and focus on the creative process and the marketing of your goods. It's nice that you only need to transfer the artwork files and they'll often take it from there. Nevertheless, I only license to companies I would want to buy from myself. That makes for a good fit.

6. How do you decide what to work on next?

It's generally what my husband and I are most excited about; whatever we talk about the most. Right now, it's our Airbnb in Joshua Tree. It's next to a national park and we're thinking about building more houses near other national parks to create a brand for those who like outdoor adventures, but don't necessarily want to go camping.

We also think about what would be the smartest choice financially. It's a blend of the two; what would be most exciting and what allows us to have the most financial freedom?

7. How do you manage your finances when starting new projects?
Having cash to draw from when starting new projects is crucial. When we started our freelance business, we had a strong savings account to get us going for about six months. To start our Airbnb, we needed to have significantly more savings to pay for the downpayment and materials for updating the house. It's exciting that the Joshua Tree House is already profitable, so now our next goal is getting the finances to start another project.

8. What's something you would like to recommend to someone who wants to start a business such as yours?
I believe that having a hobby is incredibly important. You should always do something that's just for yourself and share that with the world. Having shared my patterns on Instagram has also resulted in some new UI/UX clients. Even though patterns and UI/UX work may not seem directly related at first, they're all representative of my style as a designer. Try to create a lifestyle, a brand, around your work. Craft your own style and give yourself the freedom to experiment.

> **"CRAFT YOUR OWN STYLE
> AND GIVE YOURSELF THE FREEDOM
> TO EXPERIMENT."**

9. What are the greatest challenges for someone who wants to get into design?
Finding good clients. You need to find clients who are on the same page as you and can communicate well. If communication goes smoothly, you'll have so much fun! We can normally tell right off the bat when a client won't be a good fit. For example, if they start off by saying something like, "We've been talking to ten designers and we want you to design two pages of our site so we can choose who we want to proceed with," that's a red flag. If they expect us to do that for free, we won't continue the conversation and you shouldn't either. When a client approaches you, they need to trust you. Otherwise, they won't ever trust you and the project

will result in more stress and frustration than it's worth. Good clients will bring you more good clients. Stick with them!

10. What resources would you recommend to someone who wants to start a business such as yours?

Social media. I've learned so much from it; we're living in an age where you can pick anyone to be your mentor. I feel like I have a lot of different mentors on Instagram and just seeing what they do and say is incredibly helpful to refine my own art. I've been reaching out to people whose style I like to ask them to meet up for a coffee, and I've been able to meet so many wonderful people this way. Become part of the community, comment on people's images, and get involved with what they're trying to achieve.

"YOU CAN PICK ANYONE TO BE YOUR MENTOR."

@saracombs
www.designcomb.com

HAVE YOUR OWN POINT OF VIEW

People often talk about how you need a niche to be successful, but a niche isn't everything. It might not be so much about your niche and the specific product or service you offer, but much more about who you are as a person. I once read somewhere that it's not skills that make people successful, but rather their ability to communicate and express themselves.

Your niche doesn't necessarily have to be something that you work on. It can be what you think, what you're passionate about, and what you want to talk about to others. Your own point of view and your personal values are what people come to you for.

The internet has enabled us to find anything and everything, so it's become much harder to stand out with something you offer. Whatever you produce can be produced by someone else, and probably at a much lower price point. The only way to escape an unnecessary price battle is by crafting your personal style and sticking to your values.

On the internet, people buy from people they like or what Google shows them first. I don't want you to compete with any kind of algorithm. Much more, I want to assure you that it's okay (and actually strongly encouraged) to be whoever you are and be interested in whatever you're interested in.

When I first saw Shayna (I know, I know. I keep cross-referencing to people you haven't met yet. I'll introduce you to everyone throughout the book in more detail. I promise.) speak at a conference, she said, "The bigger the sea, the greater the need for a guide." She was speaking about the big, blue internet.

When people, i.e. your potential clients or customers, search for something online, they have a very selective perception. If they get tired of searching, they'll ask others for a recommendation, which could be you! The internet is about people and communities that are connected based on their interests.

The internet is a tool to connect with people with similar lifestyles, opinions, and values, so being open about who you genuinely are will make it easier for others to find you and relate to you on a personal level. People, clients, and customers don't just want a designer, copywriter, or illustrator; they want someone who values something specific, who has an opinion, has an audience with particular interests, or has a style they admire that aligns with theirs.

Having your own style and opinion will make people come back for more. Creating just one product and hoping it will sell simply isn't enough. You need to show up repeatedly and look at what you're interested in from different angles. It will take time for like-minded people to discover your work, but be comfortable knowing that you're in this for the long haul!

If you think about what you stand for, you'll also have to think about who you want to address with your work and values. Your audience is the key to your personal success, so think about how you can add value to the people around you, to those you want to address with your work.

When I talked to Elaine, she said people need something specific they can relate to that makes a connection with you. Later, when they need to find someone to help them with a specific need, you'll be the first person to come to mind. This is also why you should never take on clients that don't align with your personal values. Every client is a reference for future ones, so if you have unappealing clients, you'll get offers by more unappealing clients. Don't set that kind of trend for yourself! This is where your side project plays another important role; it's a quick fix if you want to shift your business or change the type of clients you work with.

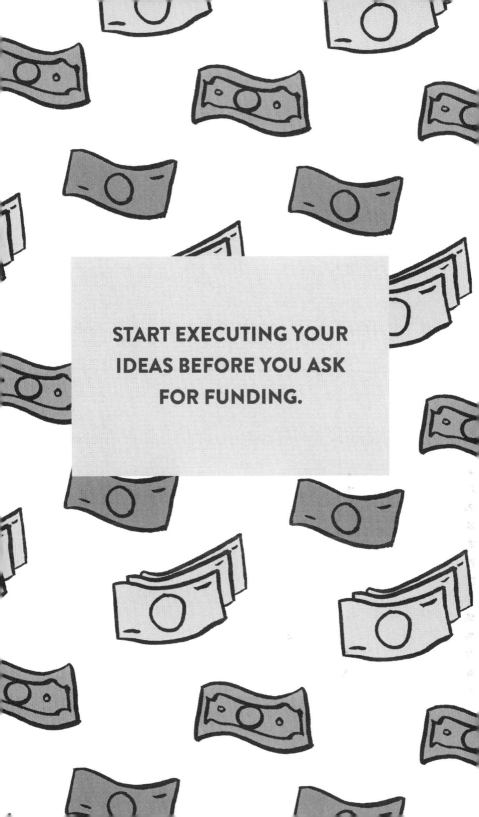

START EXECUTING YOUR IDEAS BEFORE YOU ASK FOR FUNDING.

Just as everything does, your point of view can change, shift, and evolve over time. If you think about who you're addressing with your work and how others will benefit from working with you or buying from you, then what you produce will grow and shift with the needs of your audience.

If you have a personal standing and interests that genuinely excite you, it will not only be easier for you to create out loud, but also to open up to people who might find value in your work in the long run.

Elaine, for example, has an incredible approach to connecting with strangers and turning them into friends. She actively seeks out people with similar interests and connects with them over the projects she's working on in that particular moment. Her projects align with her interests, so people who enjoy seeing her work once are much more likely to support whatever she works on in the future. It's simple; if people find your point of view and your angle on something interesting once, they will find it interesting again. And if you find a way to add value to their everyday lives, they will definitely come back for more!

Elaine McMillion Sheldon

Elaine is a documentary filmmaker, a visual journalist, and a media artist. She works on projects from the generally overlooked perspective.

Read more about how she seeks opportunities by considering how to add value to people's lives and become inspired by how she repurposes the material she no longer has a need for.

⊙ **Appalachia, USA**

1. What's your educational background and how did you arrive to where you are now?

As a little girl, I had a fascination for storytelling and I enjoyed writing stories that I made up. When I was seven, I got an audio recorder and began spying on our neighbors. My stories quickly became more real, so it wasn't such a surprise that I chose to become a journalist. Nevertheless, my idea of what it meant to work in that field was very traditional. I thought I would graduate and start working for one of the major broadcasters.

When I graduated, it was 2009 and because of the financial crisis, there were no jobs. All the companies I wanted to work for were either shutting down or decreasing their staff. At that time, I felt very burned by the system. I was bitter because I did everything I was told to do, from earning the highest grades in university and being top of my class in high school, to doing all the internships I was told were right in order to get where I wanted to be. I finally got an internship at the Washington Post, but after only four months, the department was cut in half and I was one of the people asked to leave.

Without any money or plans, I moved back to West Virginia and took on a low-paying job at a local newspaper. I was determined to keep building my skills, so I started their social media channels and also became active on Youtube. I basically created my own job within the company and I think that was the moment when it clicked; it was up to me to figure out what I was going to do.

On the weekends and during my lunch breaks, I spent hours in the state archives to search for a story for my first feature. It dawned on me how important it is to have my own point of view and I decided to go back to school. Besides my personal projects, I worked at a production company as an assistant to the CFO during my master studies. Back then, I was disappointed not to be a part of the creative team, but from today's perspective, I would recommend to everyone to seek out work experience on the administrative side of the industry they want to break into. Personally, I've gained so much from learning how to write business proposals and pitches to museums and broadcast outlets.

My studies and internships taught me to worship my own perspective, which I think is crucial given how corporatized media has become. I also realized how important it is to build an audience.

Having a fascination for stories that had more questions than answers and seeing people who resonated with what I was working on, I stopped looking at the world in terms of what people could hire me for. Instead, I began focusing on what benefits my work would bring to people. How I could add value.

> ## "STOP FOCUSING ON WHAT PEOPLE
> ## COULD HIRE YOU FOR.
> ## INSTEAD, THINK ABOUT HOW YOU CAN
> ## ADD VALUE TO THEIR LIVES."

2. What are your different income streams?

I've always been someone that's never quite satisfied with what's in front of me. I always want to build something new; I like to start things, mostly out of my own self-interest. I figure that if I enjoy something and if I see a need for it, then there will be other people that do too. I produce work where I look at how people will benefit from it, but my initial idea always comes from within.

For the past year, one of my major income streams has been built on what I've learned from directing *Hollow*, a documentary dedicated to exploring the issues and the future of rural America. On one hand, I organize screenings in towns across the United States and I also offer workshops at colleges and universities. The financial crisis might have left a mark on me because I've learned that while there might not be any money for the media industry, there will always be money for education.

When I go somewhere to showcase *Hollow*, I charge a screening fee and then the accommodation and travel costs are taken care of by the institutions that host the sessions. Additionally, I offer workshops that are based on what I've learned from producing *Hollow*. There's the possibility to book a session where I explain what it takes to make a documentary. In this workshop, I go through all the steps that are necessary to produce a documentary and then I have exercises prepared where the attendees can work on their own ideas. The other possibility is to book a workshop where I help others plan their own documentary. This is a non-linear and highly interactive session.

Each of these workshops take half a day, but many like to combine them and book my services for the entire day. Sometimes, it's easier to get my foot in the door when I first pitch to do a screening because screenings are cheaper. Once people see the value of my work, they might be willing to invest in my workshop too. My idea is to offer something at a lower cost before I pitch all of my services to them.

I believe that when you have something unique to show, it becomes easier to build various services around it. When you have your own perspective and you create something people resonate with, you might be asked to act as an consultant.

Consulting assignments pay much better compared to producing video content. But, of course, none of these gigs fall into your lap easily. I started with sending out a bunch of cold emails and calling people. Whenever I start a project, I draft a plan and think about what groups might be interested in learning more about the content I produce. I think of specific departments at universities and approach them directly.

Generally speaking, it's important to decide what you want to stand for and what topics you're excited about and want to explore further because these concepts will be the foundation for your future assignments. Every time I work on a project sparked by my personal interests, I make sure I include an educational element that will invite people to connect with me.

Of course, it's important to remember that when you work on such intense projects, it's hard to pursue other personal projects. During the time that I was focused on explaining the concepts behind *Hollow,* I had no capacity to start another project of comparable dimension. If you're a freelance filmmaker, you can't just make a movie and move on; it's important to also take the time and distribute what you've created, at least, if you have the same educational approach as I do and don't have a team to take care of the distribution of your work.

Besides taking on screenings and teaching opportunities, I'm regularly involved with other production teams and together with them,

I work on video content for various brands and publications. They're projects where I'm not the one responsible for the overall budget, but rather work as the production assistant or the producer.

Because I often shoot material I don't implement in the final movie, I started uploading the surplus material to Story & Heart, which is a licensing platform for video footage. And not to forget, I also earn money through royalties from a T-shirt idea I once had.

All in all, I earn money through video assignments I take on, screening, teaching, and consulting. I also make some money through the stock video footage I produce and then some extra dollars I receive from the T-shirt sales. I'm also the producer of the podcast series *She Does*, which doesn't generate a significant amount yet, but that income has been on the uprise because we were asked to become part of Slate's Panoply network and they arrange commercial partnerships for us.

3. Why and how did you launch your different businesses?

I think I decide on what projects I pursue based on four things: Does an idea stir a reaction in me? Would I be willing to pay for it myself if someone else did that? Is it an idea where I would be bummed if someone else would do it instead of me? Do I know where to find the audience who's interested in what I decide to produce?

To give you some practical examples:
Many of the businesses or the initiatives I started are launched around projects I've worked on. The consulting business, the screenings, and the workshops came out of producing a successful documentary that people wanted to know more about. Initially to materialize *Hollow*, I applied for funding at different institutions and approached various people and organizations whose mission was aligned with ours. I also ran a successful Kickstarter campaign to fund the project.

During the screenings when people introduced me to the audience, they would say I was from "App-a-lay-shia." I thought it was funny and decided to make a T-shirt to teach people how to pronounce "App-uh-latch-uh" properly. Everything I produce is usually intangible, so working on a physical product and trying to understand how it could work was good enough of an argument for me to play around with the idea for a couple of days. As a freelancer, I'm fully responsible for how I spend my time, so I give myself the freedom to dedicate time to projects like this.

The Appalachia T-shirt was meant to be a joke, but I sold out of the 100 shirts I produced within one single weekend. It wasn't a long-term project. I fiddled around with Photoshop for a couple of days, looked for a local printer and a producer of T-shirts, set up a free Big Cartel webshop, connected it to my PayPal account, and figured out a bulk shipping deal with USPS. After I sold out the first run, I ordered 500 more T-shirts and sold out of those too. Then, a local museum contacted me with the request to sell them the T-shirts in bulks before they asked me to sell them the idea. I negotiated a contract where I get a cut of the earnings as long as they produce the T-shirts. The first offer I received was to get a down payment and a cut of the profit for the first year, but that didn't make any sense to me. It will forever remain my idea, so I negotiated a percentage until they no longer want to produce the T-shirts to sell them. So yes, you can even turn a joke into an income stream.

She Does, the podcast I co-host, was founded because Sarah Ginsburg and I wanted to listen to such a podcast ourselves, but couldn't find one that met our expectations. At this moment, there might be a misconception in the earning potentials of podcasts because even though we're part of a network that supplies us with ads, there hasn't been much money coming in. On the other hand, we only began in January 2015. What I've learned is you can't give up on things too early. If you're excited about something, figure out another income source that will supplement the project until you find a way to monetize it.

Being consistent is probably the most important learning. I would even say consistency is the theme of my professional life.

4. What would you say are the skills you capitalize on?
Flexibility! I used to think being multi-disciplinary was a disadvantage. I used to think one had to be exceptionally good at one thing and one thing only. But when you think about it, there's no longer a factory in all of America where people could do just one thing. I personally be-

THINK ABOUT HOW YOU CAN ADD VALUE TO PEOPLE'S LIVES.

lieve that when you train people to become good at one thing exclusively, you're setting them up for failure. The economy is changing every single day and you have to be capable of adapting and mastering whatever challenges you face.

Also, I'm not scared to try new things. Sure, I'm not a podcaster, but I'm not scared to try it. It feels good to know I'm trying to produce something I'm not 100% comfortable with, and I do so week after week. When I think of *She Does*, I know it's not as good as what I like to listen to myself, but I can only improve if I keep putting it out there.

Another thing I've benefited from a lot is I've trained myself to interview myself about my own work. By forcing myself to speak about my work out loud, I've learned to talk about what I do with others. We often write what we do on a piece of paper, but it never sounds as natural as when we say it out loud. I know there are people who produce creative work and are able to live off of that, but I would say it's advisable to learn how to talk about what you do. If you can somehow work some educational aspects into your work, you'll be much more likely to make a living with your creativity.

We tend to feel arrogant when we speak about what we've done and achieved, but what I've learned from facilitating *She Does* is that explaining how someone got from A to B, or from A to C is what really inspires people. It's not arrogant at all, but rather extremely helpful because others can benefit from the information that might otherwise not be accessible to them.

5. How do you attract new clients?

I never approach anyone with just an idea. I invest time, research, and allocate resources before I pitch to brands or institutions. I shoot photos, I conduct interviews, and sometimes, I already have some sort of a trailer for what I envision to produce. I make sure I have at least 10–15% of the work done already.

I've come to understand that when you pitch to a national broadcaster, they're not too enthusiastic when project ideas don't come from within their own organization. The bigger an organization, the faster they can make something happen than you, so I'm a little more weary before I present. I make sure I have something that will make me indispensable. Instead of throwing around millions of ideas, I dive into a project and really show I have what it takes to accomplish it.

> ## "THE SECRET TO ATTRACTING NEW CLIENTS IS A FORWARD MOTION. DON'T JUST PITCH IDEAS; START EXECUTING THEM, AND ONLY THEN ASK FOR FUNDING!"

I believe if you only pitch ideas without ever making anything, you won't get very far. If you wait for someone to hire you for something as vague as an idea, I don't believe it's very likely they'll give you the funding you need. On the contrary, if you prove you can do a little bit yourself, that's going to make you credible to whomever you want to have as your partner that you can actually accomplish what you propose.

For example, the way it worked with Mashable was we only pitched to them after we finalized about 30–40% of the project. They joined forces with us and invested resources to finalize the design and the technical part of the project.

I also go to various film festivals and conferences that I'm interested in, but as you probably know, conferences are very expensive to attend, so I apply to speak at various panels instead. You just have to be creative and if you want something, find a way to work around what you consider a challenge.

6. What's your process when working on a new documentary?
It all starts with creating Google alerts and various spreadsheets. I make lists of all the news articles that have ever been written about the topic I'm working on. I take the time to at least skim through every single one of them and highlight the people mentioned. Then, I create a separate spreadsheet to collect names of potential characters, which I then research. I look whether they still do what they were doing when the article was written and I also research their contact details. I then approach them and ask for a pre-interview to check whether they're interesting as

a character for the documentary. Only then will I go to see them in person; sometimes I film them, sometimes I just go to spend time with them to better understand their surroundings before I even pull out a camera. When you make documentaries, you need to be comfortable observing. What matters most is I set myself schedules and deadlines.

When I was working on setting up the Kickstarter campaign for *Hollow*, I set Google alerts for related keywords, such as "rural America," "Appalachia," or "rangering." Afterwards, I would connect with all the people I found to let them know about my upcoming project and that I would be fundraising in the foreseeable future. It was great because I had a list of 200 people I knew were interested in the theme even before I went live. Even better, I didn't ask them for money immediately. When I eventually published my campaign, I followed up with everyone and although not everyone contributed, many of them retweeted or told others about the project.

Because my work is densely about places and people's environments, I go to the locations and spend a week there. I book an AirBnB or a hotel room and I write down what I consider unique and interesting. I go to the mayor's office, the local school, and all the other trusted institutions. I try to become a trusted person and attach a face to what I'm doing. In small towns, the word spreads rather quickly, so if I manage to be on the good side of the superintendent of the school, for example, then usually things will work out just fine.

The production process is always rather long and messy. It requires following stories and being comfortable with not knowing where these stories are going. And throughout all of this time, I'm usually constantly busy writing proposals and raising money.

When I was working on *Hollow*, people in the area often pointed me to other people who earned money from the natural resources in West Virginia. I put together a proposal and met them for lunch. I explained what my plan was and what I intended to do with the money I had hoped to receive.

You have to look for strong partners, NGOs, or brands that have the same mission as you. Non-profits usually have a community fund and from my experience, they're trying to get rid of the money at the end of every year to not make any profit. When I pitch to these institutions, I always choose the arguments that serve their community. I research what these organizations have invested in in the past, what type of projects they support, and I try to find a way to fit into their existing program. I make it as easy as possible for them. I continue what they already do and try to take work off their shoulders instead of adding more to their already busy schedule.

My recommendation is also keeping a calendar with interesting events and deadlines so you know what's coming up and where you could apply for grants.

Whenever I work on a movie, it's not that I just have a dream, find a story, and then make it without thinking about the distribution, the audience, and the financial side of the business. While I'm out shooting, I'm also constantly thinking about editing. It's a very entangled process.

When I started working on *Hollow* and received the necessary funding from the Tribeca Film Institute, our Kickstarter campaign, and through personal donations, I was able to hire seven people to work with me on the documentary full-time for eight months. Once the documentary was released, I had dissolved the production company and started a consulting company to facilitate workshops and screenings. Once you're finished with shooting and editing, you have to take care of the distribution.

With everything I do, I try to build systems to scale my efforts. Every time I finish a project, I take the time to reflect on what worked and what didn't and I learn from my mistakes. If a pitch isn't successful, I adapt based on my learnings and I try again. It's really important to not just do things once and simply try again. Take all your courage and try to fail one more time, but try again with a system. Having systems also works when you pitch to others to work with you or give you money; why should they trust you if you don't have a system in place? So even if you don't have a defined system just yet, try to build your work processes as if you had one. You can let people know you're flexible and can adapt your system, but have a base plan for what you set out to do with their money and their time.

Another part of making a movie is applying for awards. You heard me correctly; for most awards, you must apply and even pay to be considered. When I was looking where people with similar work got their funding from, I kept wondering how they received all these awards. When I found a project I really admired that won five awards, I researched every single one of them and learned not just about the application process, but also the fees needed in order to submit your film. I made a list, another spreadsheet, of all the awards of projects I respected and noted the budget I needed to apply for them.

When working on *Hollow,* I had a list of all the awards applicable to the project. I decided on the most important ones, allocated a budget, and applied. It was an incredibly proud moment when we actually became nominated for an Emmy award in 2014. I remember us sitting together, amongst people from PBS, CBS, ABC, HBO, CNN, New York Times…you can just imagine! All the people with huge institutional support and I looked around and felt so much pride for having worked with people who didn't have any support but each other's. We were putting everything on the line. Today, I can't even imagine working for anyone but myself, but I also know I have to be the one who submits the applications for the awards I want.

7. What do you outsource and what do you do yourself?
For me, everything starts with an experiment. I first do a lot of work by myself, mostly the preparations. But then, I outsource everything that takes too much time and where I know others have more suitable skills to accomplish the tasks better and faster.

I no longer hire through online networks. Instead, I ask around and have people give me recommendations, but even if it's friends of friends, I have contracts with everyone I hire where I specify they have the rights to promote the work, but they don't own it.

I usually outsource editing if it's going to take more than a couple of days because I know these days are valuable to get new work. But then, of course, it depends on the project I work on. For *Hollow* where I was responsible for the entire project, I hired people as soon as I knew my budget. When you work on a personal project, it takes a lot out of you because you're fundraising, distributing, and sometimes, I even feel like a social worker. I've learned and explored what's possible while working on *Hollow,* so I know that for the next project, I'm able to identify what roles I need to look for; people who will become strong partners and help me make a better documentary.

Once I allocate a budget, I hire people for a longer period of time. I also work with people on continuous projects, like with the illustrator of our podcast series, Christine Cover, who gets paid for every illustration she creates for us.

While I almost always pay everyone I work with, I sometimes barter skills too. With the sound designer of the *She Does* podcast, I spend a couple of hours on the tasks he doesn't enjoy and build his contact list or look for possibilities to have his projects exposed to a wider public while he spends time improving *She Does*. Sometimes, I even barter with clients if what they can offer me serves my needs better than the money I would receive.

I also outsource the sales of merchandise because even though they get a cut of the earnings, they usually sell more than if I did it myself.

8. What resources would you recommend to people who want to break into your industry?

For starters, I would say you should look at the people you admire. Google what awards they've won and what fellowships they've received and then research those too. Make yourself a list, start a calendar, and keep notes of when different fundings are usually due. I'm not saying this for you to follow other people's footsteps. I just think that people's biographies are a great resource for when you want to learn more about the possibilities available to you.

Personally, I consider the Tribeca Film Institute to be an incredible resource; they organize workshops and provide filmmakers with educational material and information about funding. MIT's Open Documentary Lab offers free events and their Docubase is a mind-blowing collection of documentaries.

I think that it's not just important to produce work, but also to consume what's already out there. Get inspired by pieces others have produced. Sundance Doc Club's streaming service is a great resource if you're curious about the work of filmmakers that's lesser seen. And, of course, if you're a woman, Chicken & Egg Pictures is a great resource because they only support female filmmakers. Schedule an appointment with them and pick their brains! They're great!

No Film School and IndieWire are great resources. You can find lists of funding opportunities and they keep lists of film festivals too.

On another note, a great resource for finding new stories is my Facebook feed. I'm Facebook friends with the majority of people that I portrayed, so I discover stories in the status updates they might not even find that significant. Then again, it's a mistake to think you'll find the most incredible stories online because once it's online, someone else has already written about it. Go out, leave your laptop at home, and talk to the people you meet. Everyone has a story, so talk to people and find it.

9. What are the greatest challenges for people in your industry?
I would say it's the best time to be a filmmaker because there are more possibilities than ever before. I have friends who produced a low-budget series, uploaded it to Vimeo, and then were approached by HBO. They literally started with zero budget and now their work is shown on HBO. What I believe you really need is a unique perspective, your own opinion, and the courage to stand by it because there's a lot of content out there and everyone is fighting for attention.

And then, I would say you should be careful with what you promise. Try to put a system in place for what you can deliver so you also have a realistic timeline. Establish systems to replicate what has worked in the past. For example, if you have received funding from a non-profit in the past and what you delivered was perceived well, try to replicate it when you apply for another funding from a different organization.

"CREATE A SYSTEM FOR YOUR WORK. REPLICATE WHAT HAS WORKED IN THE PAST."

10. What advice would you give to someone who wants to start out in your industry?

Often, when people start freelancing, they have this misconception that they'll only do whatever they decided to make the focus of their freelance career. But from what I've learned, that's never the case unless you're extremely established and have editors and agents sending you new assignments every single day. In other words, be flexible.

Also, I don't live in the expensive hubs like New York or LA. Many might think that's a disadvantage, but editors talk to people from these cities every day, and if you have a different background, you might be able to provide editors with a different perspective. I still go to the cities a lot because it's harder to find a community where I am, but I choose to pay rent in places where it's affordable. Editors usually think I can tell them something authentic because I see the world from the perspective of someone who lives in Tennessee, so you can even use that to your advantage!

I would also recommend cutting your expenses and invest your money in projects you want to work on. It will be a long-term investment in your future. I promise!

@emcmillion
www.elainemcmillionsheldon.com

CREATE OUT LOUD

Part of working on your business as a solopreneur is being your own marketeer, as well as your own salesperson. It's a lot for a single person to do, given the day has a limited amount of hours.

When I talked to Patty, she told me that everything she does, from writing an email to going to a networking event, is marketing. That's very true; however, not every creative wants to spend time talking about what they do. It might be you want to spend as much time as possible creating, so it's important to find ways that market your creative business while you're busy producing new work.

I personally believe the easiest way to market a creative business is by getting into the habit of creating out loud. What I mean by that is you need to find ways to leave digital breadcrumbs all over the internet to lead people to your website and email address so they can easily get in touch with you.

Not everyone feels comfortable using social media, and many seem insecure about how they should be using it to market their work. The best way to market your work is by sharing it on platforms that are relevant to your business. As a visual creative, it might be Instagram, Behance, Pinterest, Shutterstock, EyeEm, or another stock database if you want to build a passive income stream along the way. If your business is built around your opinion, you might want to share on Youtube, Twitter, or bookmark your articles on Contently. Finding the platform you feel most comfortable with is important. It's unnecessary to be everywhere. However, the more breadcrumbs you leave, the more people will find you.

While some platforms are more suitable to share your progress, such as Instagram or Twitter, other platforms are great to help you market your finished work, such as Behance, Contently, or let's say Creative Market if you produce something that multiple people find useful.

Having a website as a freelancer is a must, but you also need to share your work on platforms where people search for specific content. When you share your work, you, of course, need to make it discoverable too. You can either display your style amongst others or use appropriate hashtags that will lead people to your creations.

Some of your digital breadcrumbs will help you market your business, while other breadcrumbs can become products you can monetize. I was incredibly impressed when Maaike told me she uploads all the surplus work clients don't buy from her to Shutterstock and makes extra pocket money from that. She basically monetizes her online portfolio! What a smart chick!

The way I found Ewelina Dymek, the illustrator of my first book, *This Year Will Be Different*, was by searching "portrait" on Behance. Given she hashtagged her drawings, it helped me find her amongst other illustrators whose style didn't meet my taste as much as hers. Sara, on the other hand, was asked to commission her illustrations because she participated in #The100DayProject and shared her illustrations with her community on Instagram. Someone liked the designs she produced and asked if they could use them for their own products. And Maaike gets client requests regularly because people find her work on Shutterstock and like her style, but want something unique for their brand.

When you think about where to market your work, think about where other people in your branch showcase it because that's where potential clients will look. If other illustrators, designers, or writers you associate with use certain hashtags, use them too. If you have a personal style, then it's your style that will make for the final decision.

Personally, I take a lot of pictures with my phone throughout the day. Some I share on Instagram, but there are many pictures I take that aren't too personal to me that might be just what someone else is looking for. In 2014, I started uploading pictures to EyeEm and gave my approval for them to sell them as stock. I take these pictures anyway, so why not monetize them?

Think about how to be resourceful with your creative output. Of course, you can buy hard drives and hide your work, or you can just upload it somewhere where it can become an extra income stream. If you have a unique personal style, it will be a portfolio that will make you money on top of everything else.

When you finish reading this book, you'll learn that everyone I interviewed has built multiple income streams to support their businesses. As a freelancer, you trade your time for money, but as a creative entrepreneur, you make sure to have several income streams to support your business. The internet has given us many possibilities to create and let other people sell our work; whether you produce something specifically for a platform or just use what you already have that's good enough for others to make use of, don't hide your work in the dark. Bring it online to use it as breadcrumbs that will lead to future assignments, like Maaike does. Her practice still amazes me!

Maaike Boot

Maaike is a surface pattern designer and an illustrator specialized in motifs targeted at children and young adults. Not only is she working with various global clients, but she has also built a significant portfolio on Shutterstock that helps her generate a scalable income.

In her interview, Maaike explains why leaving your laptop behind and hitting the road to travel can be the best decision you'll make to keep your art fresh and your perspective unique.

📍 **The Hague, Netherlands**

1. What's your educational background and how did you arrive to where you are now?

I've always been creating things, so studying something that would eventually lead to a creative career felt like a logical step to me. I chose graphic design because it seemed like a major I would be able to monetize. On the other hand, illustration felt more risky.

During my studies, I missed making things with my hands, so I decided to do my masters in typography. I was fascinated by all the different shapes and the rhythm of letters. I still missed drawing, but I did that in the evenings and on the side.

I worked as a graphic designer at a company that specialized in designing stationery goods. When I learned about Shutterstock, I started uploading my illustrations I had created in my free time. This was in 2007.

Back then, people didn't like working with stock and the people who contributed to the platform weren't too professional. It was a risky move. However, it made more sense for me to upload my patterns and illustrations to Shutterstock than to keep them in a drawer or on a hard drive. It's important to keep your work where others can see it.

I saved the money I earned selling stock to have a solid foundation for when I decided to quit my full-time job. Before starting my own studio, I worked in a few different companies for six years, some partly during my studies.

It took me about six months from when I decided to go freelance to finally have the guts to quit my job. At that time, I was fed up with the stress and the responsibility that wasn't paying off. With freelancing, every accomplishment feels like your own.

2. What are your different income streams?

I earn the majority of my income through direct client assignments. Every time I work with a client, I present them with three options to choose from. To get to these three options, I create about ten total, so whatever the client doesn't buy, I upload to Shutterstock. That's also the only online platform I use to sell stock. By now, I've uploaded about 3,000 patterns and illustrations. From time to time, I get requests for existing patterns, but then I'm asked to tweak the patterns and sell exclusive rights on the adapted illustrations. That's great too.

Many of my clients find me through Shutterstock. They like my style, but they wish to receive original art. You could say I use Shutterstock as an online portfolio to showcase my style and my handwriting, and simultaneously, I monetize it. Sometimes, I get collaboration requests through Facebook. Social media really is a great tool for potential clients to find your work.

"SOCIAL MEDIA IS A GREAT TOOL FOR POTENTIAL CLIENTS TO FIND YOUR WORK."

I have a few clients I work with regularly. My patterns are very suitable not just for stationery, but also for phone accessoires, fashion, bags, underwear, etc., and every time I travel, I find my patterns used for something else. I've lost track of what my patterns are actually being used for! That's also the risky part of selling stock images: you never know what people use your creations for.

Whenever I'm in between clients, I might create patterns for stock, but I don't work with everyone who approaches me. I like to choose who I work with, so sometimes I just use the time I have to work on patterns that have been on my mind for a while. I always have an urge to create. I'm definitely not fast enough to make all the illustrations I would like to, and even though stock might be a very slow business to be in, it might gradually pay off for you.

3. What do you do to grow your business?
I consider myself very lucky to be in a business that's very visual. It feels natural to use social media and show my work. I use Facebook, Instagram, and Pinterest to grow my business.

In a way, I grow my business whenever I upload illustrations to Shutterstock. I don't have goals I want to reach every month like other fellow designers who work with stock that aim to upload around 150 new images every month. Sometimes, I have more time and it can happen that

I upload 60 new illustrations in a month, but other times, I don't upload anything for months.

I believe in order to grow my business, I must continuously produce work that remains fresh. I have to stay ahead of the trend and make art that goes with it. Even though I like to create unique designs, I adapt colors and shapes and I choose patterns I believe could sell as stock.

I'm also planning to expand my business by seeking out collaborations and partnerships. That's my next step. For example, I'm trying to set up a line of fabrics. My goal is to find someone who can take care of all the logistics and administration. To me, finding good partners to focus on the non-creating parts means that while I might not earn as much since they get a cut from the earnings, I can remain independent and do the parts of the work I enjoy the most.

4. How does it work for someone who wants to start selling illustrations and patterns as stock?
I would say you need to get to about 1,000 patterns uploaded to Shutterstock before you'll notice an income. First, you might be able to afford an extra beer from your earnings and then maybe, at some point, an extra dinner with friends. It's a very slow and gradual growth. The more images you upload that are relevant to the buyers, the more money you can make off of stock.

It's important to remain on trend. Do your research and look for what's still missing in the databases. If you want to become a successful seller, it's important to produce things that are popular or haven't been illustrated and uploaded to a stock database yet.

I like to get inspired by all the other industries. Fashion is a great one because fashion designers are way ahead of others. If you notice something's popping up in fashion, it will probably soon become a major trend. I'm not necessarily referring to retail stores. I like to look at fashion magazines because they're usually two years ahead of what sells in stores. A couple of years ago, I spotted pineapples for the first time being used in photography in Brazilian, Spanish, and Australian magazines. I decided to create a pattern with pineapples and uploaded it to Shutterstock. When you research and know the industry, you can predict what will get a global trend. Years later, smaller brands started using that motif and it's been last summer's best selling print.

Whenever I'm abroad, I like to pick up local magazines. Sometimes, my friends that live abroad send me magazines they think I'll enjoy, and that really helps to stay on top of what's trendy in the world.

Every country has a different style. For example, Germany is a market that's still very colorful, but the US prefers more of a Scandinavian style. You can use that sort of knowledge to remain relevant to the markets you want to serve.

5. How do you organize your work days?

Whenever I'm at home in my studio, I start the day with a list of things I need to do and complete that first. I'm most creative in the mornings or late at night. Luckily, I have the freedom to work whenever I want to. If I look outside and it's sunny, I'll go out and enjoy the weather, make photos, or go to a museum during a cold day for a new dose of inspiration. I just make sure to work every day until at least 1pm. Usually from about 10am to 2pm, I'm crazy productive, but that's also something I can't plan. At the beginning, I used to work throughout the times where it was difficult for me to focus because I was so afraid I wouldn't be making any money to keep me afloat. But now that I've built a client base and a portfolio of stock images, I feel far more at ease to take a break.

I spend about two months traveling each year. I remember the first time when I was packing and decided to leave my laptop at home. It was scary at first, but now I never bring my laptop with me and it's great. I schedule my Facebook updates and just bring my camera with me.

> ### "WHEN YOU GO ON HOLIDAYS,
> ### DON'T BE AFRAID TO LEAVE YOUR
> ### LAPTOP AT HOME!"

However, even when I'm traveling, I'm always switched on and looking for inspiration. I always see something I can use in my work later on, but in that very moment when I'm out and about, there's no way for me to create.

Everything I do always starts with this light bulb moment. It starts with little words, little ideas, and then I start drawing. Then again, I might not like the shape or the color and the inspiration passes as quickly as it showed up, so I have to ditch what's in front of me. It really depends on my mood. My work is a combination of how I feel, how I want to express my feelings and experiences, and I also look at it from the buyer's perspective to consider what will sell.

6. How do you decide what to design next?
It's a mix of things that sell very well; trends I see are evolving and trends that are coming my way. When I go to the beach and notice something that catches my eye, like some shells or the form of sand, I might get inspiration from there.

When I first started, I used to create one-off drawings, but now I create series because I've realized many buyers have no technical skills and they appreciate when I give them several options with slightly adapted details and color options.

If I see something I created years ago picks up again and suddenly starts selling, I'll adapt the illustrations and add more variations. I've learned that trends are changing fast, but because of the technology that's available nowadays, buyers don't need to pre-produce their products years in advance anymore. Things happen faster and people adapt to trends quicker. It's important to remain informed and know what's popular and trendy, so keep that in mind when creating new work!

7. What would you say were the milestones for your business?
Back in the day, starting out on Shutterstock was something I did to remain resourceful. It was an incredible honor to receive an invitation from the team at Shutterstock to meet some fellow creators. I realized they took me and my work seriously. I even won an award, Shutterstock Stories Grand Jury Prize, a few years ago.

Shutterstock is a very anonymous platform: you just upload your work. People you don't know buy it and you don't even know what they'll use it for. Also, you'll only receive a few cents every time someone buys one of your images. It doesn't feel like a big deal, but when I was able

EVERY DAY YOUR WORK
FILLS YOU WITH JOY
IS A MILESTONE YOU
HAVE ACCOMPLISHED.

to meet other creators and the team behind Shutterstock at their NYC headquarters, that was a great acknowledgement.

I really love that by continuously creating work I love to create, I'm actually making a living. That I'm independent and can do the kind of work I love, I would say it's a huge milestone every single day.

Focusing on serving my clients and creating stock images on the side makes my business feel very stable. There are no real highs and lows. I feel as if my business could just grow steadily. One of the highs was when a company from Belgium asked me to design an entire collection. It was my favorite store that I loved going to while studying in Belgium, so it was a great honor! I actually think they found me through Shutterstock too. They probably liked my style and had enough references for the quality of my work, so they reached out.

And, of course, the biggest milestone, the biggest achievement, is that I see my designs pop up all around the world. Anywhere I go, I always see something I've created. Wherever I travel, be it to Japan or Spain, a piece of me is a piece of that place too.

8. What's something you would recommend to someone who wants to start selling patterns?

Become a good researcher and take the time to look at different cultures and the styles these cultures prefer. Keep your work real, honest, and make sure it's yours. Don't copy! Have the guts to have your own handwriting! Figure out what you like and keep true to yourself. It's the only way your work will be recognizable and different.

**"HAVE THE GUTS TO HAVE YOUR
OWN HANDWRITING, YOUR OWN STYLE!"**

Focus on expanding your business and think about the long run. If you upload ten patterns to Shutterstock or to any other stock database, don't expect it to make money instantly because it won't. Every royalty-based business is an investment that will pay off gradually.

9. What are the greatest challenges for someone who wants to become a professional surface pattern designer?

Don't expect to become a millionaire. I personally think creative people don't need a lot of money as long as they're able to remain creative. Sometimes, being an illustrator means you'll treat yourself to a bottle of champagne and sometimes you'll have the cheap wine from the supermarket. Just stay focused, keep creating, share your work, and be resourceful with your creations.

10. What resources would you recommend to someone who wants to go into surface pattern design?

There are many online learning platforms that can help you become better at your craft. Shutterstock offers Skillfeed, there is Skillshare, Udemy, and many others.

If you're just starting out, don't buy anything that's ridiculously expensive. You really just need a piece of paper and a pencil. Your smartphone is good enough for you to take a picture, which you can then upload to your computer and vectorize using Illustrator or another software that converts pixels to vectors.

And then, don't hesitate to share your work on social media. Don't be afraid of copycats; this will always haunt you, but they can never copy your talent and your unique style. These people can never copy how your style will evolve; you're at least three steps ahead! Share what you create!

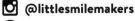 @littlesmilemakers
www.littlesmilemakers.blogspot.com

SET YOURSELF GOALS

Let me set the record straight here for a second. The difference between being a creative entrepreneur and being an employee is that as an entrepreneur, you need to be proactive and set your own goals. Not just goals, but deadlines too. And because you're the boss of your own company, your goals must fit your needs and your lifestyle.

Whether your goal is to have more clients, better clients, more followers, more sales, or more visits on your website, you should always make your goals figurative and set a realistic timeline to reach them. Once you determine figurative goals, you'll be able to break them down to smaller goals and feel like you've accomplished something important each day. Consider it your job to give yourself reasons to celebrate. I usually have a champagne breakfast (Viennese style; I'd definitely go for Bloody Mary's in NYC) with one of my freelance friends whenever I have some good news, and so should you!

If you're a solopreneur, you'll receive only a minimum of external triggers. No one can promote you or promise you more money to motivate you to reach higher. It's in your hands to figure out where you're headed because every single day you get up, there may not be any external tasks waiting for you.

Say you're only starting out as a freelancer or you want to work freelance as a side hustle. It's very unlikely work is coming your way day in, day out. For the majority of the time at the beginning, there's no one thinking of hiring you, so the day is all yours. If you don't set yourself goals, you might quickly feel disappointed about the lack of interest in your availability and either retreat to platforms that promise to help you find low-paying jobs, or start looking for full-time employment all over again.

If you have the financial freedom to spend more time on side projects, do that because building a stable business requires you to think of different approaches to monetize your skills. My personal suggestion would be to not only focus on what services you can offer to others, but to also think about how you can package your skills as digital products. Whatever it is you do, there are always several possibilities to make use of and monetize your skills. You can either find a platform to monetize your creative output, set up an online store, or teach a class on a platform, such as Skillshare. Use the time you have to explore different ways to create multiple income streams. Many possibilities are mentioned throughout the book, but I'm sure that there are many others we haven't come across yet.

When you have specific goals, it will be easier to analyze your progress, improve your skills and your business, and also feel accomplished. What I found most impressive when talking to the gals for this book was how disciplined they were, how they always knew what they were working towards, and how they knew exactly when it was due. It pays off to sit down and map out what you want to work on and accomplish each week, or even the entire month.

Your goals shouldn't be just about how much creative output you want to produce, as it's mentioned on several pages in this book. You should also set goals for how you want to work *on* your business. Maybe you want to have more people link to your website or mention you in their blogs. You might want to meet people within the industry, so you determine a number of professional networking events that you'll attend each month. Whatever it is, always attach a number for what you plan to accomplish to be able to tick it off your list once it's done. Then, pop the champagne.

Remaining positive is especially hard if things aren't going as planned. Sophie talked about several moments when she couldn't even afford a zucchini in the supermarket, so whenever things are especially challeng-

**YOU NEVER KNOW WHAT
WORKS FOR YOUR BRAND
UNTIL YOU'VE TRIED.**

ing or whenever you feel like you want to reach more, you need to keep a cool head, push through, and work harder to reach your goals. Also, set new goals once you're about to finalize a task to keep moving. We'll talk about long-term goals later, but for now, get yourself a cup of coffee and enjoy your time reading Sophie's interview. I found it incredibly inspiring and have a hunch you will too.

Sophie C. Ryba

Sophie is a savvy businesswoman who knows that being in business means you're never satisfied. There's no finish line, as you'll always find something that you'll want to improve, iterate, or update! Sophie is the founder of *TheLipstick*, a blog dedicated to beauty, Cosmeterie, an e-commerce business for cosmetics, and she also co-organizes the biggest lifestyle blogger conference in the DACH region. No big deal.

In her interview, Sophie explains how to decide what direction of your business to proceed with and when it's time to discontinue income streams that no longer work.

⊙ **Vienna, Austria**

1. What's your educational background and how did you arrive to where you are now?

I've always known I would become an entrepreneur, so studying economics felt like a degree that would enable me to do just that. When I graduated, I wanted to move abroad, but because I finished university right at the peak of the financial crisis, I couldn't find a position anywhere outside of Austria. Instead, I got an internship with Estee Lauder. They offered me a full-time position after only six weeks.

My father is an entrepreneur too and he said I needed to work for a corporation before I could work for myself. He believes that one needs to have the experience of working for a big company, so I followed his advice. After exactly one year and one day, I quit.

My plan was to start an online beauty magazine and I thought I would be a millionaire in about a year, which, of course, didn't happen! As we learned in university, I wrote a business plan and described what I imagined my company would be like. I now know that a business is an ever-evolving organism. Your business plan isn't a reality, but an imagination and while it's important to have one, you must be willing to iterate.

"BE WILLING TO ITERATE!"

I saw a potential in starting *TheLipstick* because there was nothing comparable in the German-speaking countries. I wanted to start out big, so I took out a loan of €30,000 and registered a GmbH, which is comparable to the American Inc. You need to have a lot of cash in your bank account to be able to start a company where you're not personally liable. My approach was to invest the same way as you would when opening a physical store. However, online, you can easily start small and iterate as your business and your following grows. You're getting constant feedback.

Even though I made it my business to pay my loan back quickly, it put a lot of unnecessary pressure on me. Retrospectively, it might not have been the smartest decision to take on a loan before I had a proof of concept. I don't think it's wrong to think big, but I think you should start out in a way where you don't have to run after every customer in order to pay your bills. You should be able to choose who you want to work with and who is representative for your brand.

"FIRST, GET A PROOF OF CONCEPT! THEN, EXECUTE!"

I started *TheLipstick* in 2009; it was meant to be a beauty directory and discussion board. One of the features of the platform was my blog. However, I never intended the blog to become what it is today. It was fascinating for me to see how most people visited my blog and didn't pay much attention to the rest of the website. Remember, 2009 was way before blogs became a thing in the German-speaking market, which made me realize there was probably a great potential, so I decided to become more serious about blogging. When you looked at what was happening in the US, they were already miles ahead. At the beginning, I wrote about personal things. People came because I shared my personal opinion and that was an incredible feeling!

What I completely underestimated is when you run a company, you also have to earn money. Of course, that sounds ridiculous, but back then, it didn't occur to me that clients don't knock on your door just because you're there and available!

It took years until brands were willing to spend money on online advertising. However, it was easy to build a following because there was no competition, so while I had a lot of readers, I didn't have anyone interested in paying me for the community I built. Not in the beginning anyway. But because I worked in a corporation before, I knew what they were looking for, so I managed to convince people to pay me. After three months of hard work, I received my first paycheck. It was a proud moment, as you can imagine! Even though the amount was close to nothing compared to today's standards, it was still a big accomplishment.

2. What are your different income streams?
I probably have three or four different income streams. I also have someone who helps me to make it work.

On my blog, I book advertorials and some affiliate links. Affiliates don't really make much income in my opinion. I've also built an online platform, Cosmeterie, to help beauty stores from the high street, with their e-commerce presence. It's a dropshipping business because they still carry out all the logistics and I just get a cut from their earnings for doing their online marketing. I also work as a social media consultant and I co-organize the first German-speaking blogger conference. It's an honor to be consulting big corporations that work with PR agencies and often have someone in-house run their social media channels.

3. Why and how did you launch your different businesses?

When I first started *TheLipstick*, I emailed everyone I knew and told everyone I met about my latest endeavor. I asked all my friends and family to forward my flyer to people they thought might be interested. I used my network on Facebook and I've done millions of things to get a better Google rank; I posted on other forums, created new content every day, and linked my new articles to older ones for people to stay on my website for longer than just a few minutes. I also commented on other people's blogs and sites not only to let them know I liked what they were working on, but also to get a back link to my own blog. It's like leaving digital breadcrumbs.

I had my beauty directory, but the majority of my visitors went directly to my blog. There was a forum, but hardly anyone has ever shared anything there. I then implemented a shop to my blog. I was trying out different things. It was very hard for me to explain what I was trying to achieve with my business. Today, I know that if you can't explain what your business does in one sentence, something is going terribly wrong.

> "IF YOU CAN'T EXPLAIN WHAT
> YOUR BUSINESS DOES
> IN ONE SENTENCE, SOMETHING IS
> GOING TERRIBLY WRONG."

When I eventually decided to re-launch *TheLipstick* to better meet my customers' needs, I had to get rid of a lot of features I had paid a lot of money to build. That taught me people care about good content and great pictures, not complex technology. If you're about to start something online, employ simple technologies you can use without needing help every so often. It will spare you a lot of hustle and a lot of money.

Also, part of the re-launch was that I outsourced the shop and started Cosmeterie, an e-commerce platform for small business owners. There's no exclusive content on Cosmeterie; it's an online store. In return, *TheLipstick* has become a content platform. I have weekly columns I dedicate to different topics; "Clean Monday" is about removing your makeup, "News" is where I cover industry stories, and "Beauty Talk" is where I focus on makeup tips. This is where I use affiliate links because if my readers like a certain type of lipstick, they can buy it immediately.

I've been working in the beauty industry for more than seven years, so I know the difficulties of the branch. Compared to other industries, there's a lot of potential for growth online. I had the idea to launch Cosmeterie when I talked to a shop owner at an event. I told them about *TheLipstick* and they pitied that I didn't sell any products there. I realized how much potential there was and that I could help shop owners.

The next day, I called up three people and because all of them were immediately excited about my idea, I started building Cosmeterie. My customers on Cosmeterie can rent virtual shelf space and we provide the necessary infrastructure and help them with their marketing.

Every time we onboard a new shop, we offer a three-month trial period before signing a long-term contract. We also say it needs six months to see results because people must get used to the possibility that you suddenly offer to them. We upload all products to the webstore and then we charge a monthly fee. Depending on the size of the store, it's between €70 and €300, plus 10% from every sale they make.

I don't think Cosmeterie would've been so successful from the beginning if I hadn't had my blog and all the experience from before. Establishing relationships with people who can eventually help you succeed is always a great investment in your future. When rebuilding my blog, I lost a lot of links to my website, but having people support my new project really made all the difference and I'm grateful for that.

In 2011, I met Maria Ratzinger for the first time, an incredible Austrian blogger and PR consultant. We met on Twitter during a time when no one in Austria was using the service. We found out we lived nearby, so we decided to meet up for a coffee. We immediately clicked. She was working on a blogger conference, The Fashion Camp, and asked me if I liked to get involved. I loved the idea and I'm still excited to see the blogger scene evolve year after year. If you have a chance to start an industry meetup, do it!

"INVEST IN PEOPLE. THEY'LL HELP YOU SUCCEED IN THE FUTURE."

4. How do your clients find you?

With *TheLipstick*, I have my own outlet that's simultaneously a great reference for my work. I've never gone out to look for clients. Instead, I've made it my business to make a name for myself in the local beauty sector. I go to a lot of events and that's where you meet people. If you can summarize clearly what you do and communicate it in a way to let people know what you could do for them, they'll remember you and follow up. I've had moments where people asked me whether I knew a beauty blogger who could help them and I would laugh and say I was one. You'll know if you click with people on a personal level. If not, it won't be a fun project to work on anyway. And if sometimes a client decides to no longer work with you, if you do it right, it's just about saying you have capacities and then your network will refer new clients to you. Being in business is very social.

With Cosmeterie, it's different. We actively approach shop owners and offer them our solutions. For Cosmeterie, I have an employee who takes on a lot of the things I don't want to be doing off my shoulders. She also reaches out to new stores.

When you're self-employed, you need to learn to find people to help you. You can't do everything, but you can make a list of things you need to do, make priorities, and outsource everything that's not crucial for you to do yourself.

**CHANGE IS PART OF
RUNNING A BUSINESS.**

At the moment, the clients we serve with Cosmeterie are people from the region. Whenever we pass by a cute store, we walk in and talk to them. When there's an industry fair, we visit and go to every single booth and talk to the owners. Sometimes, but it's still very rare, people approach us directly and ask us for help.

Don't forget that not every customer you win will stay with you forever. Change is part of running a business and your solution probably won't work for everyone, so don't be disappointed.

5. What do you do yourself and what do you outsource?

I never work on projects by myself; I really enjoy teamwork! Every project I work on, there's at least one other person involved. For *TheLipstick*, I work with a freelance editor; for Cosmeterie, I have an employee who's with me part-time; Fashion Camp is a collaborative project. We all have our tasks we are responsible for. I'm responsible for budgeting and everything finance-related. I know that I'll, for example, never do any press outreach. When we split up responsibilities, everyone picked what they prefered and whatever no one liked to do, we decided to do together. That's why it works so well!

It's really important to me to work with people who have a drive, but also people who don't consider themselves too important to hand out flyers or write email newsletters or post to discussion boards. If you want to know whether a strategy works or not, you must test it. I want to work with people who are curious to figure out the right solution. That's, at least, what I look for when hiring people. I've had good and also bad experiences with hiring. That's probably why I consider a probation period so incredibly important. When hiring, I like to ask the applicants if they can deal with stress, if they have a hands-on mentality, and what they want to achieve for themselves. It's important to have a mutual vision because in startups, there are no job titles. Everyone has to do just about anything.

6. How do you budget for marketing measures?

It's different in every industry, but generally speaking, for every euro you spend, you should get five in return. What I believe is most important is to think about your target group and what they read, where they go; analyze where they spend time and try to reach them there. You'll have to experiment a lot, so try to schedule one new experiment a week and set a budget for that. I've done things that have worked, such as partnering with bloggers, and then things that didn't show any results, such as getting into print magazines. You never know what works for your brand until you've tried.

"DO ONE NEW EXPERIMENT A WEEK
TO MARKET YOUR OWN BUSINESS."

7. How important are seasons in the e-commerce business and how do you handle them?
Holidays, such as Christmas, Valentine's Day, and Mother's Day are important for trade, so you have to be prepared and think of something special. August, on the other hand, is a month that we always take off because people are on vacation and no one's shopping for cosmetics. Breaks are important to gain new energy. Take some!

8. What are the challenges for someone with an e-commerce store?
You need to find your niche. If you want to position your store well on Google, you need to have a long tail business. Even huge brands, such as Louis Vuitton and Gucci, are now selling online, so there's a lot of competition. You need to think about what you do differently. How do you want to distinguish yourself from what everyone else out there is already doing; do you offer your products at a lower price? Is the quality of your products better? Or do you give your customers another reason to visit your webstore? If price isn't what distinguishes you from others, then you need to find something else and position your marketing around your uniqueness.

I would also say that having a budget is important. Many people underestimate the importance of earning cash. When you run a business, it's like a big experiment that sometimes costs you less money and sometimes it costs more. You make mistakes while you try yourself out at being self-employed, so I would recommend having a solid savings account so you don't have to jump on every opportunity, even the ones that don't feel right. You don't want to embarrass yourself and ask to borrow money, and I've had some moments where I couldn't even afford a zucchini in the store, so please calculate your budget from the beginning!

"IT'S NORMAL TO MAKE MISTAKES WHILE YOU TRY YOURSELF OUT AT BEING SELF-EMPLOYED."

9. What's something you would recommend to people who want to start a business such as yours?

Don't give up. Set yourself goals and try to achieve them. Let's say you want to have more readers for your blog. Then go out to other places and try to draw people to your site. I've had nights where I sat behind my computer until 6am to answer posts in other forums to make people aware of my existence. I would also look up groups on Facebook that talk about my topic of interest.

At the beginning, and sometimes even today, I spend countless hours approaching companies to ask them for their products that I can give away on my blog. If you want to achieve visibility for your blog, your e-commerce store, or any kind of business on the internet, you need to invest time and get involved with other communities. You'll probably deal with a lot of criticism from people who might not have the slightest idea where you're coming from and everything you've already tried, but follow your line! Be authentic and think about what you want to achieve and try out different things to get just that! As long as you really want something and you're dedicated to getting it, you have what it takes to eventually get there. As an entrepreneur, you need to learn to get up and continue. I've had so many visions for my business and sometimes, I think I'm only still here because of my endurance and my conviction that this is what I'm supposed to be doing. Many people have said to me I was being brave because I was self-employed. I've never seen it that way. I've just always known that I'm going to make it and build my own successful company. It's normal to have doubts. But then, pick yourself up again and get back to work!

"IT'S NORMAL TO HAVE DOUBTS. BUT THEN, PICK YOURSELF UP AGAIN AND GET BACK TO WORK!"

When I first started, I worked from home, but then decided to get an office. That increased my productivity, and I also no longer felt guilty when I wasn't working. At the beginning, I was incredibly insecure and often unsure whether I could manage to pay the rent for my office each month, but given how much more I managed to get done, it really paid off. The first few months where I was able to pay my bills without heavy outbreaks of sweat whenever I received mail was an incredible milestone for me. Beginnings are difficult. It takes time to establish a routine in your business.

The internet is changing quickly and different strategies work for different people; guest blogging, webinars, Twitter, Facebook ads – there is no set recipe to making your business a success. You need to try everything and some of what you try will stick and others won't. Being a businesswoman means you're not scared of iterating and trying new things!

I would also recommend starting a mailing list. The best thing about email is you can track where people click and what they're interested in. You can learn a lot from such insights.

Social media helps a lot too. You must be on Facebook and also look for a second social media channel to represent your company. If you want to go into e-commerce, Instagram and Pinterest are your best choices these days.

I also wouldn't underestimate online ads. It's a bit of a hustle because you have to read so much about how it works, but Google offers an online course, which I would definitely recommend. If you identify your target group, it will be easier for you to not only set targeted ads, but to also make the right decisions to serve your audience and your customers better.

What has also helped me grow my business is blogger relations. Look for bloggers that are relevant for your business and work together with them. It pays off to have bloggers onboard, so put money aside and book a campaign with them. Try to book several articles with one and the same blogger because people tempt to remember something once they've seen it several times. It might seem expensive at first, but it will help you see your product staged in an authentic way. The best thing about online marketing is that it never disappears. It will always be available through Google and it will forever link to your website and help you get a better ranking.

I would recommend setting monthly goals of what you want to achieve and then reflect how many hours you spent working on it to analyze whether it was worth it. Once a month, I make an analysis of the different projects I work on and I look at the earnings. It's important to regularly check how things are working out for you. And then, sometimes, kill your darlings and try new strategies that might work better for you and your business.

10. What would you recommend doing if you notice that your business isn't working out the way you expected it to?

It hurts to see the idea you had and considered brilliant isn't being well-received. It took three years for me to accept that the original *The-Lipstick* format I spent so much money on to build wasn't interesting to people.

Of course, you put a lot of effort into your business plan and it feels like a slap in the face if people don't enjoy what you thought they would, but that doesn't mean you've failed. Running a business means you're open to change. I would recommend looking at the parts of your business that work and are well-received and expand them. I noticed people liked my blog and my webshop, so those were the two areas I tried to expand further. I would also recommend thinking about what you're good at and offer your strengths to consult people. I never intended to go into consulting, but that was what helped me pay my loan back.

If you look at your budget, you must be honest with yourself because numbers don't lie. You're running a business and this is a phase.

That's okay. Map out what works and what doesn't. It's pointless to continue doing something that doesn't work. If it's not your complete favorite, don't stick with it. Stop wasting your time on things that obviously don't do it for anyone. This is a moment to be honest with yourself. Of course, when you run your own business, it's never perfect because you can always find something you could improve. But try to improve the things people find interesting and then emerge in them!

@thelipstick_net
www.cosmeterie.com

TAKE SMALL AND BIG RISKS

Admit it, one of the biggest risks you've taken in your life was probably quitting your job to freelance. At least, it might have felt like the biggest risk at the time. It might be that quitting is the one risk you're currently being confronted with, but you're still hesitant; do you take the jump or not? Whenever you decide to take a chance on something important to you, it's a sign you believe in your skills and you trust yourself enough to master the situation, regardless of what happens next. Taking risks has to do with trusting your gut feeling.

There are times in life where we must take responsibility for other people before we make decisions that will serve our personal needs best. However, if you feel confronted with the question *"What if...?"* every day, it may be time to act on your wishes. If you're unhappy now, what's worse than remaining unhappy for an eternity? You clearly need to make a plan for change. And do it for you.

In life, you take small and big risks. Taking big risks means putting everything on one card and hoping it's going to work out the way you imagine. On the other hand, small risks are just gradual steps towards your ultimate goal. There's always the chance that things might turn out completely different in the end, but it will still enable you to move towards your vision of who you are and what you want your business and your life to become. To put things into perspective, you don't need to risk it all to explore new options. However, you should take small steps in new directions regularly if only because changes and risks are inevitable when running a successful business.

As a solopreneur, it's completely up to you what you do with your time. If you don't like something, change it. You can pivot your business to suit your needs better and everyone around you will be okay with it. We tend to put too much emphasis on what other people think about our actions, but truthfully, the majority of people are busy worrying about how they're being perceived themselves. They don't have time to focus on what you're doing day after day, so don't worry about them; it's your life and you need to do what you need to do. It's okay.

Whatever the risk is you confront, it's one you'll have to overcome at some point. While I interviewed Jaymay, she said she believes if you pour all your energy into something, after a lot of hustling and a lot of pushing, it will work out. Whenever Elise faces a situation where she must make a big decision, she imagines the worst possible consequences and if they're bearable, then it's a risk worth taking.

There are several different, and sometimes scary, risks. We might fear something as small as saying "No" to a potential client who doesn't feel 100% right to you. It's natural to consider what you would get paid for a job well done, but would the job be as well done if you were truly passionate about the client? Probably not! So while this everyday risk of running your own business can sometimes feel like a big chance, it's not. It grants you time to look for new, better, and more suitable clients.

If you say "No," what's the worst that can happen? Is the outcome bearable? Yes? Then go ahead and say "No" so you can focus your energy on what feels right. Start a side project, go out and network, or follow up with the people you've previously worked with and enjoyed the experience!

Another risk that might make you feel slightly uncomfortable is approaching someone you have yet to turn into a friend, or at least a friendly contact. If you ask me, you don't have much to lose because at the end of the day, the person you admire is just another human being. They're a human being that, just like you, has someone they admire and might be a little intimidated by too. If that doesn't give you more courage to reach out to them, you should Google my blog post, "Why you should send a letter to a person you admire." You can also tweet the person you think is awesome and tell them you liked their recent piece of work. I strictly believe people deserve to hear more compliments and get regular invitations for coffee!

Then, there are risks that go beyond bravery, such as financial risks. This isn't a place to talk about investing in property, the stock market, or anything down that alley. It's about investing money in your creative projects and thus, the future you imagine for yourself. Even if you're a designer or a consultant, you should still calculate a marketing budget in your rates. Just like any business, you need to market your services to be able to work on personal projects at least once a week, if not more regularly.

When I first started investing in my business, it was by writing my first book, *This Year Will Be Different*. Not only did I invest a tremendous amount of hours into making an idea a reality, but I also had to allocate finances to pay an editor, a designer, and an illustrator. I wrote the book at the beginning of my freelance career, so as you might remember from the introduction of this book, I had no actual savings at the time. A sudden request fluttered in for a job to be done over the weekend, so I took a chance and poured everything I earned in that moment into a personal project. Given, you're now holding my second book, you can imagine realizing that project has paid off for me, although not necessarily financially!

If you want people to recommend your services, create something you want people to know you for. For me, writing a book felt like a good idea because I wanted people to recommend my services, my thoughts, my marketing strategies, and my writing. Given I started consulting Kickstarter on their expansion into the German-speaking market after my own campaign is a prime example that whatever step you take leads you to another step in the future. You need to put your energy, focus, and excitement towards something you believe in. Your secret or not-so-secret wish is always worth taking a chance on. Even if it doesn't work out immediately, it will still lead to something else that could be just as great, if not better than your expectations. If it's not, you wouldn't be pondering about it as you're most likely doing right this very second. Am I right?

Write down what you wouldn't dare to risk just yet and think about (small) steps to bring you closer to reaching your goal. Even if for now it feels unreachable, there's still at least one chance on the other side of every risk.

Chances, the exceptional and exciting side to every risk, are what will take you further in life and in business. If you, maybe not today but tomorrow, can see the chance behind the risk, the fear will eventually melt away or feel manageable.

It's hard to write an article on risks because risks are very personal and different to everyone. What I believe you should keep in mind are the consequences that make you feel uncomfortable and to then focus on what could take away your discomfort and work towards that. To me, the scariest thought has always been the question "What if?". If I think about "What if?" and "Maybe..." and "How could that be?" for too long, I feel like I'm wasting my time. I'm not actually accomplishing anything, just thinking in circles. At that point, I try to break down big ideas into small, actionable steps and work hard to make it feel less risky. Practice solves everything. And for now, for you, practice starts on a sheet of paper where you can break down big ideas into achievable steps.

I hope you find the power to face the risk that scares you. And even more, I hope you see the chances that are waiting for you out there. For now, enjoy Elise's story.

Elise Blaha

Meet Elise, a creative entrepreneur who started with a small Etsy shop she grew into a viable business. Her most successful product has been the *Get To Work Book ®*.

One of Elise's incredible strengths is her ability to look at risks from a very pragmatic angle. She'll explain why it makes sense to start small, and why it's important to think about who you are and what you stand for in order to build a business that can flourish and grow with you.

📍 **San Diego, USA**

1. What's your educational background and how did you arrive to where you are now?

I've always been interested in business, so I studied business administration. I chose marketing as my major, but since I studied before social media was a thing, everything we learned was different from how you market today. (I graduated in 2007.)

I never thought I would start my own company; I was sure I would work for a corporation. During my time in college, I had internships at about six or seven different companies. I gained a lot of work experience, but never really clicked with anything. I can't say I didn't like any of these jobs; it was just that none of them felt like something I wanted to stick with.

In my senior year, I interviewed with a lot of companies all over the United States. None of them offered me a job, so I moved to Maryland to live closer to my now husband. I took on a retail job at a paper store where I earned nine dollars an hour. Even working full-time, I had a lot of extra creative energy, which is why, next to my blog, I started an Etsy store.

I started my blog in college in 2006 when blogging wasn't big. I used my blog to share personal stories and my craft projects, and my audience grew gradually. When I started blogging, social media wasn't really there yet, so the only way to grow your audience was word-of-mouth from your readers.

When I decided to start an Etsy store, I was lucky I already had a small audience from my blog and invited everyone to check out what I was up to. Originally, I created single products, but eventually focused more on creating lines. I started to treat my Etsy store more like a "real" business.

I worked at the paper store for over two years, but as my Etsy store (my side business) started to grow, I was able to cut back my hours and focus on building my own business. It was wonderful because it happened slowly. I always had a stable income more or less, or at least some income.

2. What are your different income streams?

Currently, my biggest income stream is the *Get To Work Book*®. It's a daily planner and goal-setting workbook.

About 10–15% of my overall income is generated through affiliate links on my blog. I also have some DIY e-courses that I sell through my website and on A Beautiful Mess. The e-courses on abeautifulmess.com are distributed by their in-house staff. I get a share of the income.

Additionally, I sell some other products next to the planner on elisejoy.com. And from time to time, but definitely not regularly, the podcast I'm working on has a sponsored episode here and there.

3. Why and how did you launch your different businesses and your different products?

I started with a small Etsy shop first and in 2012, expanded to selling rubber stamps. This was the first product I sold via a free-standing shop instead of through Etsy.

In 2014, the year I turned 29, I wanted to rediscover my footing as a maker and figure out what could be next for my business, so I came up with the project Make29. I decided to produce and sell a new product once a month for twelve months in a row and release these creations in batches of 29 or 290. It was a series of limited editions for me to figure out what I enjoyed making the most. During this year, I sold photo prints, screenprinted posters, letterpress prints, and wooden plant stands. I also created knit blankets and various paintings.

Make29 was an experiment in selling and an exercise in goal-setting and following through. I would recommend to everyone who wants to challenge themselves or really get better at something to experiment! I learned a lot about product development and how to run my business more effectively while operating on the monthly turn-around. I was really hoping that by making all these different products, one of them would click and I could then make it the base of a full-time business.

Some of the products did better than others, but what actually happened was I received a lot of questions around my planning process. All these questions became the foundation of the *Get To Work Book*®. I wasn't intending to create a planner; I actually thought I would write a book about goal-setting, but then I realized instead of just talking about doing something, I wanted to provide something that helped people take action.

Currently, my focus is on the *Get To Work Book*®. I launched the planner at the beginning of 2015, so there's a long way to go to really see what it can be. I worked with a great team in Portland, Oregon on the design of the book. They were able to take all of my ideas and goal-setting concepts and turn them into something beautiful and functional.

The design and production for the *Get To Work Book*® is done out-of-house. I'm currently handling the shipping, customer service, website design, and promotion. Eventually, I would like to outsource the shipping.

My goal for the *Get To Work Book*® brand is not to over-expand or create hundreds of products. I want to just have a few, consistently good products that sell. I now have three products and I would love to get to about ten over the next few years.

One popular page in the *Get To Work Book*® is a project breakdown sheet, so I plan to launch a notepad and book based around that design for people who have a lot of projects, but may not need the daily planner aspect. I think taking a huge financial risk (the big planner) and then three small financial risks (the notepad and two small products) might be a good rhythm for me. If one of the three products doesn't work out, I'm still in good shape.

I think I spend the majority of my time thinking through the business side of a product and then the creative side happens quite fast. Ideas come quickly, mostly while I work on something else, but setting up logistics...that's the real hustle.

For the future, I would love to sell wholesale. I would love for stationery stores to stock my products, but for that to happen, I need to go to gift and trade shows. There's always something new that's worth exploring when you run your own company.

4. How did you set up the logistics for your business?

I work with spreadsheets and calculate. First, I always do a cost analysis: if I order X amount, I have to sell Y amount to break even. I must know

EVERYONE STARTS FROM SCRATCH AND GETS TO WHERE THEY ARE NOW, AND SO CAN YOU!

the numbers and think about whether it's a realistic amount and if it makes sense for me to realize such a project.

I don't consider myself an inventor. I know many people like to innovate, but I prefer to figure out what already exists that I can tweak and make work a bit better. That's how I channel creativity; I look for solutions that are already available and adapt them to my taste.

I look for local suppliers because it's important to me that I can pick up the phone and call the people I'm working with.

I also determine how much inventory to order based on some cost-analysis. At certain order quantities, I receive a price break, so all of that is considered, as well as how much I can afford to "lose" if things don't sell and what my break even point would be at each quantity. For 2016, I doubled my order based on the 2015-2016 sell out and the assumption that more people would be willing to purchase a traditional calendar year planner.

As mentioned, right now I'm doing the shipping for the *Get To Work Book*® out of my house. For insurance purposes, I don't store all the inventory here (some is held at the printer) and instead, I have pallets of books shipped down every month or so. This allows me to manage risk and save some storage room. If things continue to grow for the brand, it will be unrealistic and impossible for me to ship everything from my house. I'm currently looking for a distributor and while it will be hard to give up that part of the business I've done for so long, it will be the right decision.

5. How do you grow/scale your business?

Every time I invest a new product, it's a risk I dare to take. When I started out with the *Get To Work Book*®, I invested about $45,000. I didn't have to pay everything in advance and was able to pay off some of the costs with the pre-orders, so I didn't spend $45,000 in one day. Still, it was the biggest risk I've ever taken in my life. By far! Before, I never invested more than a few thousand dollars, so you can imagine it was a very big move for me.

There was no safety net, but I knew we wouldn't lose our house if I couldn't make it work. I believe that in business, you must learn to separate the real problems from the unreal problems. This was a business risk, not a life risk. We'd get through it.

Because I've grown things slowly over time, I've never had to borrow money. When considering a new venture, I like to think about the worst-case scenario. If the worst-case scenario is terrible, then I don't move forward. Often though, the worst-case scenario isn't that bad.

Over the years, I've taken many risks; I've done so again and again. When your decisions work out, it gives you the strength to take a risk again. When they fail, it helps you realize it's okay. The world keeps turning and that gives you the strength to take on another risk. It's just something you learn through experience.

It now makes sense to me that many people cherish experience over education. I think education is hugely important, but still, you'll learn a lot while doing. You'll grow with your decisions and with how your business develops. Also, after you've dared a few smaller risks, it becomes less intimidating. But of course, it's still overwhelmingly scary.

6. How do you market your business?

Right now, I rely heavily on Instagram. Every time I send out a planner, I include printed thank you notes to encourage my customers to share a picture using the hashtag #gettoworkbook. I have a *Get To Work Book*® Instagram account where I feature people's images. I try to connect with them, and instead of saying, "Here is a photo Jane took," I say, "Hey, Jane, I like how you did XYZ!"

7. How did you improve the user experience over time?

I'm still working on it. I think that's the case with every brand. There's always something to improve.

I've grown my business organically and shared my gradual process on my blog. People like to connect with what's happening behind the scenes and that's helped. I've also implemented a newsletter and connect on social media.

I work to be responsive to customer needs. My customer service model basically goes like this: "Make it right. If people want a refund, okay, I'll give them a refund. If they want puppies, sure, I'll give them puppies!"

There will always be a reason for customer frustration. That can't be avoided. But once they voice their frustration, you can do something about it and fix it.

8. What's something you would recommend to someone who wants to start a business such as yours?

I believe it's hugely important to realize that building a business isn't quick. Part of why it's worked for me is because it's been so slow. I didn't set out to have a huge business. It grew purely out of my interests.

The first step you should take is find out what you're interested in. It doesn't have to be anything that sets you apart. It just has to be something you're passionate about.

Then, you should be comfortable with starting small. Learn to be comfortable when you don't have a whole plan mapped out in front of you. In order to run a successful business, you need to be flexible, willing to ask questions, and staying true to who you are. Be prepared that building your own business is going to be hard work. You have to absolutely love it!

I personally love the business aspect; I love calculations and spreadsheets. If you don't enjoy that part, then find someone who does. If you don't enjoy marketing, then find someone who does. Work with people who fit with your strengths and weaknesses.

9. What resources would you recommend to someone who wants to start such a business?

I have three books that I would love to recommend: *The Creative Habit* by Twyla Tharp, *The $100 Startup* by Chris Guillebeau and *The Art of Possibility* by the Zanders.

10. What do you think are the greatest challenges for someone who wants to set up a business such as yours?

It can feel daunting to break in. It's always hard to start from scratch and start building an audience for the work you do. I was lucky because

IF PEOPLE WANT A REFUND,
GIVE THEM A REFUND.
IF THEY WANT PUPPIES,
GIVE THEM PUPPIES!

I built an audience through my blog before I even wanted to sell anything to anyone. Now, there's such an incredible hype around how many followers one has, which makes it feel really hard to start out, but that shouldn't stop you! It's okay to start from zero and grow slowly. Everyone starts from scratch and gets to where they are now, and so can you!

Take time to think about what your brand will look like and what you want to focus on. Make sure whatever you produce feels consistent. Come up with a really clear idea of who you are and what your brand stands for. That should eliminate at least some of the fears of starting out.

Also, separate your own identity – who you are – from your business. I know your personal business is a personal endeavor, but try to not take things personally. I'm still working on this myself. I now feel I finally have a product that I'm crazy passionate about, but it took me ten years to find it. I've been working on things I've been interested in for ten years that made for my income, but it's only now, ten years later, that my passion product could really be profitable and scalable.

Pursue your interests really hard and go all in. It's only by going all in, believing in yourself, and believing in your business that you'll be able to figure things out!

@elisejoy
www.eliseblaha.typepad.com

KICKSTART YOUR IDEA

By now, I've challenged (or more so encouraged) you several times throughout this book to think about your side project, an idea you would love to see attached to your name. Now, it's time to share some good news about how you can make your idea come to life.

Sometimes when you have a good idea, you have the drive to make it a reality, but maybe not the finances. Cue in Kickstarter! It was invented for that sole reason. Of course, there are other platforms out there, but given my heart belongs to Kickstarter and especially its team, I'm making this chapter dedicated to my platform of choice. However, what I'm about to say applies to other platforms too!

What I believe makes Kickstarter special is the community that helps realize creative ideas and encourages artists, designers, musicians, and other creative spirits from around the world. If you have an idea and/or a prototype that excites people, you'll eventually find the support you need to help realize your project.

One of the most important components to running a successful campaign, in my opinion, is being generous. Your project should be for and about the people you want to win to become part of your community. Running a campaign on Kickstarter doesn't only help you test your idea and see whether you know what people like about your work, but it also enables you to go public with something you haven't had to produce in advance. Additionally, Kickstarter is the perfect platform to connect with people interested in your work directly without having to establish distribution partnerships, or convince a banking consultant to give you funding for a project they might not believe will work.

When I went live on Kickstarter the first time, it was because Ewelina, the illustrator of *This Year Will Be Different*, couldn't meet her deadline. With that title, I wanted to spread the word about the book in the first week of January and Kickstarter seemed like the perfect way to do just that.

To this day, I'm incredibly grateful for that change of plans because without receiving Ewelina's sad email, I wouldn't have discovered what a powerful tool Kickstarter was and is. Back then, I launched the campaign within four days. I begged Anna Heuberger, the co-founder of We Love Handmade, to tape a video on New Year's Eve while she was cooking for a dinner party. It took us three hours to tape that two minute video (sorry about that, Anna!) and I haven't watched it since. I felt so uncomfortable! Taping a video of yourself might be the hardest step if you're like me and feel out of your comfort zone doing it, but remember you have an idea that will serve the needs of people. Do it for them!

While you can publish a Kickstarter campaign quickly, it might make sense to prepare in advance for the campaign to fund your project properly. Here, I'm happy to share with you what I've learned by not only running my own campaign, but also by helping other people launch their campaigns while working on the launch of Kickstarter in Germany.

If you want to use Kickstarter to realize your idea, I recommend sitting down and thinking about the people who can benefit from your project the most. Think about what value you add to people's lives. I would go as far as saying that you should brainstorm the rewards you want to give to people for supporting your project, even before you start writing or making a video. When deciding on what you want to give away as rewards, always think about whether you would be willing to pay that amount for such a reward yourself. Then, think if you would get genuinely excited about receiving said reward. Honestly, do you really need another T-shirt in your closet? I didn't think so. Make the reward something practical and realistically appealing.

Try to make your supporters, your backers, as involved in your project as possible. Kickstarter is a place where you can open up about your creative process to people who are interested in participating. If you're making a movie, why not collect photos from your backers and photoshop them into newspapers or postcards to show on the screen, or if that's too much effort, why not mention your backers' names in the credits? If you're making garments, why not embroider the backers' names on the inside of the clothes? See what I'm suggesting here? Involve them!

Important Sidenote: Speaking of rewards, it's crucial to note something I didn't anticipate during my campaign (spoiler alert: grab your highlighter). When calculating the costs of your rewards, please wrap the products, go to the post office, and make sure you know how the shipping costs will be different in different countries. This is probably the most important piece of advice because personally, I completely underestimated this and ended up paying for parts of the shipping costs with my nonexistent savings. Lesson learned.

There are endless possibilities to make people become part of your work and that's why people come to support projects on Kickstarter in the first place.

Of course, the video is pretty much the key to the success of a project. If the project is good enough, a simple video, such as the one I recorded to promote *This Year Will Be Different*, can also make the cut. Nevertheless, if you have the time and the resources, don't be afraid to play. People love videos that are fun and unexpected. Independently of how big your team is that you convince to help, make sure your video explains the features of your project; it must showcase how the user will benefit from using your product, in what situation your product will be relevant to them, or why it matters that they get involved. The Coolest Cooler is a great example to learn from. What I really like about the Coolest Cooler video is that Ryan managed to explain why he was the right person to realize such a project, something that's crucial given you're asking people to support you financially.

When writing copy, use images to break up the long text. Visuals always win! If you already have photos of your rewards, don't hesitate to show them.

Once you've launched your project, it's important to start spreading the word. In the beginning, you'll need the support of your friends and relatives. If none of the people who know you personally trust your abilities to finalize and deliver the outcome of your project, strangers won't trust you either. On Kickstarter, about 17% of all unsuccessful projects haven't received a single pledge, which clearly shows that spreading the word among people who know you plays a huge role.

The majority of projects on Kickstarter raise between 1K and 10K, but if you're planning to start a bigger project, you'll need to take more time to prepare your launch. Firstly, and as mentioned before, think about who might be interested in the outcome of your endeavor. These are the people to reach out to immediately after your Kickstarter project page becomes public. Sometimes, you might need the support of the press to reach more people. There are several ways to go about this. First, I'd always recommend thinking about who you know who might know someone else they can introduce you to. If your project is for your community, don't hesitate to reach out to your local newspapers. Let them know about your project. This is usually easier in smaller cities. If you don't know any journalists or weren't successful with the local media houses, it's time to do a little research. A simple hack is to go on the Google News search and find relevant keywords. When you find articles that are related to your project's theme, reach out to the journalists who wrote them and let them know about your project. If they're interested in your field, they might be kind enough to feature your campaign.

Once your page is up and running, you'll have about 30 or 40 days to reach your goal. Trust me, you don't want to shout across all your social media channels that you're doing a Kickstarter campaign and people should give you money. Instead, this is a wonderful opportunity to tell people more about your work. Take the time and write regular project updates to invite people to check out your Kickstarter page. Don't do the sales talk. Instead, talk about your progress and how your project's

CREATIVITY IS AN
ATTITUDE TO LIFE.

evolving. Give people something to talk about; show them photos of your work space or the material you won't show in the final piece. In the end, backers on Kickstarter want to be a part of the creative process, so the best thing you can do is share your work with them. It'll be easier to regularly post on your other social media channels about your campaign without constantly asking people for support. You'll see that posting project updates will be valuable even after you've successfully funded your project. As I like to say, if you've done one campaign well, it will be easier to make the second one even better.

You've already read Elaine's story; she has run a campaign to finance her documentary *Hollow*. Now, it's an appropriate time to share Julieta's.

Julieta Ulanovsky

Julieta is a graphic designer and an educated typeface designer. Together with her business partner, she specializes in creating brand identities for local clients. However, she believes she adds the most value to the creative community whenever she works on her passion projects. Julieta loves to create designs dedicated to capturing the beauty of her hometown, Buenos Aires. In her interview, she speaks about the importance of collaboration and how she gets people involved in her projects, even before they're complete.

📍 **Buenos Aires, Argentina**

1. What's your educational background and how did you arrive to where you are now?

Originally, I studied graphic design and then, 20 years later, I went back to university to study typography. I wanted to venture into typeface design.

I've worked since I was 17. In 1989, I started a graphic design studio together with my friend, Valeria Dulitzky, who I met in school. We immediately started to work on projects together and we enjoyed it so much that we continued working together on projects in university and afterwards. It's been more than 30 years since we met and we still get along as well as we did in the beginning.

We specialize in editorial and brand identity design. Even though I went back to school to learn more about typeface design, I no longer create fonts and typefaces. I loved doing it during my studies, but the technical side of being a typographer is challenging. I prefer to work together with people who take over the technical detailing while I focus on editorial projects.

A couple of years ago, I ran a Kickstarter campaign to create a font which captured the beauty of old street signs in Bueno Aires; the names of old buildings, old canopies, and the spirit of an old and beautiful city. It was a passion project and also my biggest typeface project I've ever created.

2. What are your different income streams?

Over the years, we've built a reputation within the local community, so there's always something for us to do, although, it's become a challenge to put time aside to work on projects we initiate ourselves. We've done two crowdfunding campaigns to finance two projects we really wanted to do: one was for a book about the Palacio Barolo, the building in which we have our studio, and the other was for the Montserrat Typeface to preserve old typographies of Buenos Aires. We love to work on projects that help us shed light on the beauty of the city.

It's easy to just continue working on client assignments because you know exactly what to do, but with your own projects, you're the creative director and the driving force behind your ideas. You must be a lot more self-confident about the decisions you make regarding your personal projects because there's no client to tell you they're happy and to move on. You are your own client. It's hard to draw a line with your own work because it feels like you're never satisfied.

3. How do you set time aside for your personal projects?
We try to have one day a week for personal projects for us to evolve our skill set and stay inspired. When there's enough client work coming to you, you must feel an incredible desire to do something for you to pull through and finish a personal project. Treat a personal project just as you would treat a client project to make sure you accomplish it. There's no one else who makes you finish, so the desire must come from within. Sometimes, we would love to be more strategic about the projects we decide to pursue in our personal time, but then we know we'll only enjoy the project if we get excited about the process. It's not about the money.

Whenever we have an idea, we try to find people to help us with the parts we aren't as good at. We're professional designers, but it challenges us to do the marketing. We overcome what we find difficult by involving people from different disciplines. We have a great network of wonderful professionals who help us when needed.

Getting people involved with our work is something we love to do. Before we launch a new project, we usually get feedback from people we respect. It doesn't just help us produce better work, but it also helps us spread the word because when you get people involved, they relate to your project far more.

"WHAT BRINGS THE BEST OF YOU TO THE SURFACE?"

Our long-term dream would be to focus more on our own projects, but it's hard in Argentina to make a living as a creative, so while we feel we add more value to the society whenever we focus on projects driven by our personal vision, we don't think it would be a safe choice to jump into doing that head over heels. Still, it's important to work on something you're truly excited about and where you can decide on every single detail. In the future, we want to make more books. We believe that books bring the best in us to the surface.

4. Why did you choose crowdfunding to release your project?
With our first project, the book about Palacio Barolo, we couldn't find a publishing house, so it felt like the best choice. In 2011, we used Kickstarter to release a typeface. Kickstarter isn't available to creators in Argentina, but we had someone from the US who helped us set it up.

Dave Crossland, who's consulting on the Google fonts project, visited us at the university where I studied typeface design and he really liked my project. It was his idea to use Kickstarter to not only finance the project, but to also spread the word about it globally. We weren't familiar with Kickstarter at all and trusted his judgement.

It was incredible to see people from all over the world support our project and give us money, even though they didn't know who we were. People from every continent were reaching out. We asked for $5,000 and we received almost $10,000 within four weeks thanks to the Kickstarter community.

But I don't want to mislead you; doing a Kickstarter campaign is hard because you're constantly online, responding to people's emails and replying to their comments.

When Dave suggested using Kickstarter, he wasn't sure whether it would work or not. I believe the Montserrat Typeface was the first project dedicated to typography that ever launched on Kickstarter. It was a risk, but Dave really believed in my work! He encouraged me to show my face and the way I work, so I prepared a script for the video and guided people through my office and my neighborhood. I guess the best experience I had on Kickstarter was I made really good friends with people from the industry. Harald Geisler, a Frankfurt-based typographer, was one of them. He's done some incredible Kickstarter campaigns to support his projects. He's been using Kickstarter to fund his work for years.

When you're on Kickstarter, you recognize how close the world feels. You're in contact with so many people. I still receive emails, even years later, from people asking me about the Montserrat Typeface. If you show people your art and if you publish it on the internet, people who love your work will find it and if you're lucky, they'll get in touch! If you need people to find your project while you're live on Kickstarter, you better help them find it quicker because time is limited!

5. What does your creative process look like?

Valeria and I are trying to remain very open to new ideas. We draw inspiration from different aspects of life; when we see someone in the street who catches our eye, or notice a color combination we admire. Inspiration is everywhere! It's about being open to these idea moments. I believe it's a decision to be open and creative. Creativity is an attitude to life!

"CREATIVITY IS AN ATTITUDE TO LIFE!"

But, of course, there's a difference between feeling inspired, having an idea, and deciding to turn it into an actual project. Whenever an idea becomes a strong desire, it feels like we're just here to help it be born.

If you're endlessly excited about a potential project, you'll figure out the time to do it. We're excited about our book, our office, graphic design in general, and the typeface we released thanks to Kickstarter. This is how we decide what to work on next.

Unfortunately, the older you get, the more critical you become. It's not as easy for us to be excited about opportunities that come our way, so we just realize personal projects where we don't mind that there's no direct money reward involved.

6. What have you learned from running a business for such a long time?

How important it is to be polite in everything you do; whether it's emails or phone calls. All of the team and client communication is really sensitive and you need to approach it as such. However, it's important to have your own opinion, your own standing. People could commission anyone else, but the reason they come to you is because of who you are and what you stand for. They come to you because they believe in your attitude.

You have to learn to value your work. Time is limited and you don't want people to waste it. If you don't have a good gut feeling, don't proceed with a project. Get contracts and make people pay for your work every time you reach a milestone before you continue working on the next stage.

Also, keep working on personal projects. They shape your business and help you advertise your work from an angle you want to be known for.

7. What would you recommend to someone who wants to run a Kickstarter project?

Once you click "Go live," you're in for a ride. You'll spend a lot of time answering emails. The more technical your project is, the more people will share their doubts with you. You shouldn't get angry about it. People who ask good questions will challenge you and help you become a better designer.

We were quite naive when we launched our campaign. We didn't even have Facebook, let alone Twitter or Instagram. We merely sent emails to our friends and luckily, they shared it with their network on Facebook.

We also have friends working in media who conducted interviews on TV and the radio. The project appeared in newspapers and in magazines too. Kickstarter was such a new thing, and it still is in Argentina, so it was relatively easy to get attention. However, without the support of our friends, it wouldn't have been possible.

You should take time during the campaign to be able to work not just on your project, but also on running your campaign. The better you prepare in advance, the easier it will be.

When you're planning your campaign, you should think about what you will deliver afterwards. The more organized you are as a person, the smoother it will go. When I created my campaign, I offered many different rewards, from postcards to notebooks and T-shirts. But the more diverse your rewards are, the more you'll have to coordinate and the more work you'll eventually have to manage. Everything that isn't digital has to be shipped, so you'll have to deal with wrapping many packages, go-

IF YOU DON'T HAVE
A GOOD GUT FEELING,
DON'T PROCEED.

ing to the post office with suitcases, and shipping products to countries you might not even know where they are on the map. It's a crazy experience!

8. What resources would you recommend to someone who wants to start a business such as yours?

I believe the greatest resources are the people you surround yourself with. You should get people involved in whatever you're working on, especially when you don't know how to approach something. Look for people who know better and don't hesitate to ask them for advice.

9. What do you think are the greatest challenges for someone who works in design?

The quality of the work you produce is incredibly important. For me, the key moment will always remain the moment of printing. You can create a lot on the screen, but you'll only understand what you made once you hold it in your hands.

10. What's something you would recommend to others who want to build a business such as yours?

Collaborate with others! But always trust your original idea. Nevertheless, remain receptive to other people's feedback. It's good to be open to change and implement feedback, but you should never walk away from the core of the original idea. Follow your guts, but also try to make it better by implementing the feedback you receive. Also, learn how to use Excel. That will come very handy!

🐦 **@julietaulanovsky**
🌐 **www.zkysky.com.ar**

INVEST YOUR TIME

As a solopreneur, you're held responsible for doing everything there is to do in a business, from finding new clients, to sending out invoices, to doing the actual creative work. Even cleaning your work space falls into your responsibilities. These are the obvious tasks; the ones you've probably seen yourself and your colleagues do when you worked for a company. However, what you probably overlooked is what your boss did behind closed doors or after everyone went home; strategizing how to allocate resources, what to focus on, and what to invest energy in today, tomorrow, a month, or even a year from now. In other words, it's in your hands to plan where your business is headed to keep everyone involved sturdy and happy, and to consider how your business will earn money if a client decides to end their contract with you.

Every single decision you make determines how you'll be spending your time in the foreseeable future. After I talked to the women I interviewed for my first book, I realized that as a freelancer, you can only allocate half of your time, about 20 hours a week, to client work. The earnings for these 20 hours must be enough for you to be able to do everything else that makes for a business, which isn't just the administrative work, but also the visionary work. As a one-person company, it's you who needs to think about what will make your business stable, even if something unexpected happens that temporarily steals your focus.

I've come to the conclusion that the best way to build a stable, creative business, you need to differentiate the way you make your living; if your main focus is to offer services, then you need to focus on creating products for sale. If you run a business that specializes in creating products, you need to think about a way to turn your skills into services. For you, in order to create a business that challenges you and simultaneously gives you long-term security, you need to build different pillars to support yourself.

The internet has given us multiple opportunities to scale our efforts. As a consultant or a creative, you can write books or create classes, tutorials, art, templates; there are so many possibilities you can offer for sale! You can either start your own shop on your website, or look for platforms that will sell and distribute your creative work.

Take books for example; you can use Amazon's Createspace, upload the file, and they'll take care of printing your book and its distribution. You don't need to stress over logistics because they'll do it for you! You can use EyeEm, upload your photography, and they'll sell it to agencies in need of authentic photography. You can also conduct a class on something you're knowledgeable about and upload it to Skillshare, or even partner up with a company like Casetify and have them sell your art for digital accessories. There are thousands of companies out there hungry for your talent, so it's your job to find the right ones that will take work off your shoulders and fill up your bank account while you're busy creating out loud.

I'm emphasizing on creating out loud because the more people know who you are and where they can buy your art, the more art of yours will eventually sell. While these companies that are focused on sales and logistics are great and you can bump up your sales by writing great blurbs and keywording your products properly, it's recommendable to invest time in marketing your work too. Logistic companies usually help make successful products more successful because that's where they'll earn the most money, so if you do something, tell everyone. And once you've done one product, start working on the next one! The more digital shelf space you occupy with your work, the better your sales will be, something Susan and Joanna will tell you a lot about in their interviews.

If you, on the other hand, are a creative who focuses on making products, you can commission others to help you with sales just like Helen does, or you can implement some sort of service to your portfolio of

BE GRATEFUL
FOR EVERYONE WHO
GIVES YOU FEEDBACK.
USE IT TO GROW!

tasks. Teaching people, online or offline, is a great way to connect to and grow your audience. People will appreciate buying from someone they trust. If you create products day after day, then you're probably a master of your craft and should find a way to share your knowledge. Being secretive doesn't necessarily make sense in the age of the internet because people can find anything they want online, so it's better to see your name or your brand's name attached to a technique you master. Teaching people how to do what you do isn't just a way to make an additional income; it's a way for you to market your business by creating out loud.

Now that we're thinking about how to invest your time, we should also be thinking about how not to. Chances are high you don't enjoy every part of running a business. These are the things you should delegate or outsource. Many freelancers believe they can do it all, and even if they probably can, it takes an unnecessary amount of time that could be used to work on something enjoyable to make more money and spread the word. Even as a creative, this is where you need to think like an entrepreneur. If your main income source is, for example, illustration or illustration is what you want to turn into your main income source, then you shouldn't be sorting through your receipts or photographing your products for your shop if photography isn't what you master or what you want to learn.

Working with other people who can take over parts of your business you don't enjoy or know much about will help you grow your audience if you choose your partners wisely. (We'll get to choosing partners wisely later.) In the meantime, write down what you don't enjoy doing and later on, we'll deal with who should be taking care of those tasks. Now, it's time to introduce you to Susan. I still can't believe how she makes her living. If you don't believe anything is possible after you read her chapter, I don't know what else could convince you!

Susan Schmitz

Susan is a photographer who specializes in animal photography. She gradually built her social business next to her full-time job. Today, Susan works with animal rescue groups and helps shelters find homes for their protegés by providing them with beautiful images, which she then monetizes as stock photography.

There's a lot to learn from Susan's street smart attitude to building a resourceful business.

📍 **Phoenix, USA**

1. What's your educational background and how did you arrive to where you are now?

I didn't go to college actually. I'm completely self-taught. Everything you need to know about photography or illustration is now on the internet. You can basically find anything you want to learn about or tap into resources, such as the CreativeLive. I learned a lot from tuning into live webinars and reading books and articles I found online.

Before, I worked at a mortgage company for about 22 years. I managed to quit my job a couple of years ago, but it was a slow transition. I now earn money through stock photography. You need a very solid portfolio, which takes years to build, for you to be able to live off of it.

I started experimenting with photography about ten years ago. It took me eight years to transition a side hustle into a full-time career. And to be completely honest, I wouldn't have dared the transition into freelance if my body wouldn't have suggested me to. The stress from having a job I didn't enjoy made me physically sick. I had to change something. When I quit my job and went on to do what I'm doing now, I started feeling much better.

When I started out with photography, I was spending about 20 hours a week on that. I was still working the regular 40 hours at my other job. Gradually, I switched to 30/30 before quitting my job altogether. It was a lot of hustle!

2. What are your different income streams?

My major income comes from stock photography. Shutterstock, in particular, is my main earner. There are some other agencies I work with, such as iStock, Fotolia, and Deposit Photos. Even though some income trickles in from all of the stock markets I submit, I rely heavily on Shutterstock's income. They're a good company and really look after their contributors.

I also submit to Fine Art America from time to time because I've learned that photos of food and landscapes will sell there. However, I specialize in animal photography. Fine Art America is an outlet for when I want to try something more artistic.

I usually use the same lighting setup when shooting stock images. It gives me the ability to be creative afterwards. Because of the neutral background I use, I can composite images and tell stories. I can, for example, put a chihuahua that's looking up next to a much bigger dog that's looking down. My aim is to create images for a commercial purpose, something the pet industry could find useful.

I sometimes work with private clients, but I never spend time or money marketing to them besides mentioning the service on my website. It's harder to shoot images of people because, realistically, most people don't enjoy looking at images of themselves. Animals don't complain about how they look. They don't have a bad hair day.

When I first started, I took photographs of people. I shot family portraits and people with their pets. That's when I realized I really liked working with animals. I spent more time working with animals than I did with people, so I started donating my time to rescue groups and kind of fell into the business.

When you work with rescue groups, there's no money involved. I can't charge them, so I started researching ways to utilize all the images I produced. I'd heard of some people who were selling photographs as stock. They weren't making a lot of money, but I thought that could be something I could do part-time to build a portfolio.

I'm the type of person that when faced with a challenge or a situation I don't like, I'll find a way to make it work, especially in business. I'm not a complainer.

I also have a cooperative studio I rent out to local artists. I have a partner and we split the duties. We allow renters to come and use the space on either an hourly basis, or they can sign up for a monthly program. The more they use the space, the less it costs them. It's a great way for creatives to have a studio space to work out of, which they otherwise couldn't afford themselves. The income covers our monthly rent for the studio, giving me and my partner a free place to work and a little extra cash in our pockets.

3. How do you get so many different dogs to participate in your shootings?

I work with the animal rescue community. A couple of times a month, I go to rescue groups and photograph all of the new animals they've taken in. I also have a rescue group program that allows smaller rescue groups to bring several adoptable animals into my studio each month for photographs. Professional pictures of homeless animals helps draw more attention to them, which increases their chances of adoption. It's a win-win. I offer this service for free; they find homes for their pets quicker and I get to use the pictures of these dogs for the pet images I sell as stock.

4. What does your work process look like?

I submit images to ten different photo agencies. When I first became a full-time stock photographer, I had over 2,000 images at those agencies. With this, my husband and I were able to earn enough money to get by when combined with his income.

However, it wasn't enough to live the lifestyle we wanted. I sat down and planned out my production and royalty goals for the next five years. I set out to produce 300 images per month, but that was really hard to accomplish. I wanted to stay at 40 hours a week and I wanted at least four weeks of vacation every year. After the first few months, I found out 200 images per month was a much more reasonable goal.

When I take the number of images I have in my stock library and divide the number by how much I'm making each month, I know the return per image is at about 80 cents. Some images are more marketable than others. Each image submitted needs to be high-quality and commercially valuable to become marketable and profitable. If you do the math, you can see you have to really build a big portfolio to make a good living as a stock photographer. By sticking to a production cycle of 200 images each month, my income goes up by about $160 per month. Over time, this really adds up. If you produce quality work and you stick to certain goals, you can go freelance in a couple of years.

I used to try and plan out sessions. For example, I would plan out a Christmas-themed photo shoot with a specific shot list. After a while, I

**STOP COMPLAINING!
FIND A DIFFERENT WAY
TO MAKE IT WORK.**

learned that when you work with animals, they tend to have a mind of their own. I've since given up on planning. Now, I just shoot whatever I can get. I try to get the animals into different positions for variation, then I review all the images after each photo session to determine how I want to creatively enhance them in Photoshop. As I focus on each image, I try to remember previous photos I've taken that may work well together. I can put two photos together and have them interact with one another. Creativity lies in the backend for me; it's what I do in the post-production phase. During the photo shoots, I'm just having fun with the animals.

> ## "PRODUCE QUALITY WORK!
> ## IF YOU STICK TO CERTAIN GOALS,
> ## YOU CAN GO FREELANCE
> ## IN JUST A COUPLE OF YEARS."

I label and keyword each photo properly in order to find it later. When a holiday is around the corner, I'll look through my entire collection and then look for pictures I could turn into a Christmas scene. I collage a group of different animals together and add Christmas props, that sort of thing.

I mainly work in my pajamas with my two dogs cuddled up next to me on the couch. I need to be comfortable to be able to enter my creative space. The majority of my work is editing. I love post-production. I get completely immersed in working with Photoshop. I try to have studio days about once a week where multiple rescue groups come to see me with their adoptable animals. Then, I spend four days editing the footage and pulling together what I believe will sell.

5. How do you know what images will sell?

I like to say it's common sense: if an animal is just sitting there, it won't sell well. Many buyers don't have graphic design skills, so it's best to create very specific use cases. You should think about specific industries you want to reach.

Take, for example, the grooming industry. What sort of an image will they want to use? That's what I ask myself whenever I edit images. For the grooming industry, I might take an image of an animal sitting up and put a comb and a pair of scissors in their paws during post-production. It makes it far more marketable than just having a decent image of a dog. Always think about how you'll set yourself apart from the millions and millions of images that are out there. Look up a certain subject you want to shoot. Research what's already out there and create something different.

I've also learned pictures of certain breeds sell better than others. Dogs with a black coat don't sell well unfortunately. It's also much harder to find a home for them, so if you ever consider getting a dog from a shelter, get a black one! Puppies and kittens sell very well, but I shoot all sorts of animals: snakes, alligators, tigers. I think working with animals is really exciting!

Given I work mainly with animal shelters, I can't determine what animals I'll take pictures of. For me, what comes first is what's important for the animals to get ready for adoption. Then comes my creative work. My income comes second! I believe there's a market for everything. If you label your pictures properly, interested buyers will find them. If I have pictures of an older dog, I use keywords like "senior," "rescue," and "elderly."

I now have an assistant to help me label photos because that's the part I don't enjoy. She helps me on a contract basis and takes a lot of work off my shoulders. I also like to automate as much as I can. I use Adobe Bridge because I can create a text file and then enter all the suitable keywords.

6. How does one get into stock photography?

For Shutterstock, you'll need to apply and submit a certain number of images for them to review the quality of your work. Once you've passed the review process, you'll be able to submit more pictures. iStock has an even more intense review process that requires you to pass a test. They want to know if you have the technical knowledge required to produce professional images.

I would recommend taking the tests even if you're not sure whether you want to invest your time in stock photography. Going through the approval process will really open your eyes and you'll realize how good you'll need to become and where you might have flaws in your work. For stock, you need to be technically fit.

I've learned not to take rejections personally. You'll get a lot of rejections at the beginning, but learn from it and be grateful to everyone who takes the time to give you feedback. Image reviewers are my greatest teachers because they point out how to improve my photography. I used to take it personally, but I don't anymore. They're doing me a favor by helping me become a better photographer!

> ## "BE GRATEFUL TO EVERYONE WHO TAKES THE TIME TO GIVE YOU FEEDBACK. USE IT TO GROW."

7. What do you think is important to consider when shooting for stock?

Some people that just get started in stock take whatever they find in their house and shoot it against a white background. You may get a few sales that way, but you really have to think like a buyer and find ways to make your images unique. Find ways to tell a story with a single glance.

It helps to occupy a niche so you'll become known for that area of interest. Buyers will start following your work and people will bookmark your page.

Over the years, I've built a good following of companies who buy images soon after I've uploaded them. It's good to venture off from time to time and shoot other things to keep from getting burnt out. Different subjects sell better with certain stock agencies. You can distribute images to various agencies for better sales.

8. What's something you would recommend to someone who wants to get into stock photography?

Be patient. It takes a lot of time to be successful in this business. Find a general subject and become an expert at it. But also, keep shooting other subjects to keep your perspective fresh. Try to get to know photographers who do similar things as you and make acquaintances with people who work in different areas too, to gain different perspectives.

You should also try staying on top of industry trends. Google "microstock industry" and follow the different reports that examine industry trends for you. Personally, I try to submit some images I know are trendy to gain attention from people who look for that sort of stock, but my main focus remains on producing evergreen content. I try to avoid taking pictures of modern technology, such as cell phones or laptops because they become outdated quickly. There's also the danger of fashions going out of style, especially if you capture people.

9. What resources would you recommend to someone who wants to get into stock photography?

CreativeLive has been the greatest resource for me! It's also good to look into forums, but you shouldn't get caught up in them because they can drag you down. Nevertheless, you can learn a lot from other people.

10. What are the greatest challenges for people in the stock photography market?

It's a very competitive industry. There are millions of photographs out there, so you have to strive to remain unique in your style, which is difficult. That's my own personal challenge because if you produce what everyone else is producing, you'll just add to the sea of stock photography.

You'll also need to remember that stock photography is for the long haul. You have to spend a lot of time upfront before you see a decent reward from all your hard work. When someone downloads an image of yours, you may only make a few cents, but you have to think of it as building up your investment portfolio because it's a royalty-based income. It's your retirement! It's money you can give to your grandkids. Think of the future!

@photofusionAZ

www.shutterstock.com/g/srichey

FIND YOUR NICHE

Previously, I said this guide isn't going to tell you to find your niche, so now you might be wondering how the hell I got to a point to dedicate a chapter to finding your niche. I promise I'm not being a hypocrite and it'll make sense.

The key is to not waste your time doing one thing and one thing only. Once you've sold this "one thing," you might have to look for new customers, which is always the most challenging part of running a business if you're just starting out. Don't make yourself start that process all over again!

Let's back up and redefine what your niche is. It starts with thinking about the people you serve with your work. Your niche is your follower's needs and interests!

It's very likely, and this is also something Patty mentioned, that the needs and interests of your clients and customers are probably also *your* needs and interests. If you're a mom, you might be most excited about babies, so your audience might be other moms who feel the same way. It's their problems that are also your problems that make for your niche.

As an entrepreneur, you're not someone who executes what you're being told to do. You're being hired by clients and getting paid by customers to solve a problem, so when you think about your niche, think about what sort of problems you're solving. Your niche is a diverse field you can occupy and play with. It's the problems you solve day after day that keep you on your toes and keeps the people who've discovered your work interested in what you'll do next. They'll become your audience and serving them will become the focus of your business.

When you open up on social media about the problems you wake up to solve every morning and you listen to what other people say about them, it'll be much easier for you to connect the dots and create new products and services. Your business can evolve around the feedback you receive. Even if you get stuck and feel like your mind is blocked and there's no space for new ideas, you can retreat to the comments and reactions you've previously heard about your work and the problems you've helped solve.

If you see yourself as a problem solver, than your work will forever remain relevant. If you just do one thing that's working out at this very moment, your business might one day become irrelevant. I'll give you an utterly crazy example here, but it's one you'll most likely understand because it's so well known and so obvious. Okay, ready?

Think about the *Harry Potter* series! I've read all seven books and loved them. First, I read the second book because I didn't see it wasn't the first one, and then I bought every new book once it was released. Every new book just felt right at that time because J.K. Rowling didn't write seven books for 11-year-old kids (I think I was actually 11 when the first book was published). She wrote books that were of interest to her first core readers. Every book she released was for her very first audience who became older. She didn't try to entertain 11-year-olds every time she sat down to write a book. She had an original audience and kept serving them as they grew older and evolved. The seventh book, which I got in my hands when I was 22, was incredibly dark and filled with second world war references. I wouldn't want to see an 11-year-old read that book, but for me, it was what made me buy J.K. Rowling's other books. See what she did there?

Now, look at what you do and think about who it is that might be benefiting from and enjoying your work. As a creative, you might not be an actual problem solver in the deepest sense. You might solve the problems that fit within a lifestyle, such as what wallpaper pattern suits the carpet in the living room best. So if you create patterns for wallpapers and your potential customer is dealing with finding the right carpet, you can solve their problem by either partnering up with a carpet designer and creating a collection together, or by finding a carpet producer who could commission your designs.

When you think of your audience, think of what your audience is drawn towards and where your art fits within their life(styles). Go on Instagram, look through forums, and learn about people and what they like, admire, and are genuinely excited about. Listen up when they mention what magazines they read or what podcasts they listen to and position your work within that field. Make it easy for people to recommend your work by adding value to their lives.

I, personally, love to follow creatives who share bits and pieces of their work process because it keeps me motivated to pursue the work I do. I love following people who share their techniques and are open about how they approach their everyday challenges because it helps me solve mine. And I love to follow people who go places I would like to experience for myself because it keeps me hungry for what else there is to explore in the world.

You too might have preferences and are probably able to explain why you prefer to follow some people more than you enjoy following others.

You might recognize there's a difference between keeping up on people's lives who we know and who we don't know. When we see personal photos of people we know, it warms our hearts to see their happiness, their babies, and their personal achievements. If, on the other hand, we follow the paths of people we don't know in person, it's hard to be as genuinely excited about their personal successes unless it helps us identify what it takes to achieve the goals we've set for ourselves.

If you pick your five favorite social media accounts of people you follow and jot down why that's the case, it'll determine how you could add value to others with what you share on your social media accounts. The feelings you have are probably the feelings people have when they follow you.

If you can identify why you enjoy seeing the successes of people you don't know, it'll be easier to determine what it is you should share online that's inviting others to follow along.

Share your process, create for your audience, and most importantly, as your audience grows and evolves, do the same alongside them. You can learn a lot about accommodating to your audience from Shayna. She founded a business that supports her nomadic lifestyle by listening to her students' feedback and continuously sharing what she has created for the people she decided to serve. There's plenty to take away from her story, so I hope you have a pen or highlighter in your hand!

Shayna Oliveira

Shayna, an online English teacher and the founder of Espresso English, loves her work because she can do it from anywhere in the world. She kicked off her career as an online educator when she recognized a need in her immediate surroundings.

In her interview, Shayna speaks about creating classes, products, and educational material based on the feedback she gets from her students, and how building your audience is crucial to making a living online.

◎ **Salvador, Brazil**

1. What's your educational background and how did you arrive to where you are now?

I was a chemistry major in college, but I didn't want to pursue it because you have to specialize and I have a lot of diverse interests. After a couple of internships, I decided it wasn't the career for me. I took some time off to think about what I wanted to do with my life, then went to Israel to volunteer with African refugees. They needed someone to teach them English. That's where I realized how much I enjoyed teaching!

I returned to the US to get training in teaching English as a second language before taking off again to move to Brazil, where I then started teaching English in both group and private lessons.

Many of my students were too busy to come to class consistently; they had jobs and families that demanded their time and attention. However, they really wanted to learn the language, and one day, a student who was a busy working mother asked if I could send her the class via email. She wanted to read through my lessons during her lunch breaks. I said, "Sure!" because I really wanted to help her learn English.

Once I started sending out my lessons via email, I also started publishing them as posts on my blog. I already had the content, so why not publish it somewhere where more people could access it and learn from me? I wasn't making any money doing that for at least six months, and it took about three years before I had the guts to leave my "day job" and work on Espresso English full-time.

2. What are your different income streams?

I have several income streams, but they're all tied to Espresso English. I've created nine courses, from pronunciation to phrasal verbs and business English. I've started a monthly membership program and I've also written three e-books.

Up to 30% of my monthly income comes from my bundle deal, in which I offer all of the materials and courses I've created at a discount. Once you have a body of work, you should definitely offer a bundle deal of your products.

When I first started, I chose the name Espresso English because drinking espresso is fast and that's how I wanted my students to perceive learning English with me. I wanted to give them the feeling that it's easy to learn and make progress. All of my products contain lessons that are quick and easy to complete. Whenever I produce a new course, I choose a different subject my students want to learn about.

3. How have you grown your business?

People buy courses from people they know, like, and trust. I started with blog posts and emails to people who knew who I was. You need to be patient because it takes a while to build up some traffic. In my case, it was six months of continuous publishing and about nine months until I saw some traction on my site. I also started a newsletter right in the beginning. I remember my first email went out to 12 people. Now, it's more than 50,000 subscribers, but you don't ever start at 50K. You always start with just your friends and people who know you.

> ## "BE PATIENT! IT TAKES A WHILE TO BUILD
> ## AN AUDIENCE."

The first time I decided to offer a paid course, it was because I realized that when people signed up for language classes, they paid for the course in advance. I figured I could try the same thing online. I sent an email to my subscribers and asked them what topic they would like to learn. I gave them three options: business English, travel English, and idioms. My community voted for travel English. I announced the course I was planning to run in August a month in advance. It was just a simple sign up page and the offer that they would get 30 lessons for $30.

I started producing the course once people started signing up and paying me for it in advance. I was just a few days ahead with creating the classes before sending them out to my students day after day. Once the course was over, I picked another topic and repeated the process. Although it was only a few people signing up, I could see it was working, so I continued.

For my first class, I had about 100 people who started the signup process and only 17 who made it through and actually paid. It was 17 people paying $30 dollars, so I got about $500 for a month's worth of work. I was a bit upset at first because that seemed so low compared to these super-profitable case studies of product launches you read about online. Much later on, I found out it's normal to have less than 20 people sign up for your first course. It's not too bad either because in most cases, you don't really know what you're doing. You'll only figure out a structure and get better at teaching online the longer you do it.

Although the income from my first class wasn't record breaking, I still taught a classroom of 17 students. Then, 28 people signed up for my second course. I continued producing classes for my students and over time, more people signed up. The effort I put in wasn't rewarded immediately, but it paid off eventually.

In education, the content is evergreen. Once you've done something and have done it well, you can use the content repeatedly. I'm making some changes in my courses now because there are some things that need an update.

The amount of people who sign up for my classes fluctuates to this day. Sometimes it's more and sometimes it's fewer students. It's normal to start questioning what you're doing wrong. However, I've learned the success of every class depends on my launch strategy and the choice of topic I decide to teach.

4. What's your launch strategy like?

I schedule a launch period of three weeks. I've learned when you choose a shorter timeframe, many people miss it, so I would recommend planning ahead if you want to reach as many people as possible. Having a longer launch window also gives me more time to prepare the lessons. By pre-selling the course, I trick myself into not being a perfectionist because having paying customers expecting my class on a particular day gives me a very clear deadline, which motivates me to get things done.

I offer an early bird price and then the price goes up on a determined date. That adds a feeling of urgency and people are more likely to sign up early to receive a discount. A lot of people register on the final day of the early bird period because I send an email that says, "This is your last chance to get the early bird price!". It might seem cheesy, but many people have told me they appreciated the reminder.

BE PATIENT! IT TAKES A WHILE TO BUILD AN AUDIENCE.

Usually during a launch period, I send out a sequence of emails; a mix of content and promotion. I never use high-pressure sales techniques to get people to buy my classes. It's always more of an invitation. In the first email, I announce the launch and in the second, I give away a free sample or I send out a list of lessons that will be covered in the course. I usually send out a couple of emails containing regular content where I'll just include a "PS: This course is starting soon." And I finish off the sequence with the "last chance" e-mail.

5. What's your digital infrastructure like?

When you first start out, you can use the most basic tools. I used to email download links manually, so from my perspective, Mailchimp and Dropbox are simple enough for anyone to get started with online education. I eventually changed to a paid plan at Mailchimp, and once students bought a course, they received an auto-responder with a link to download the PDF or video classes they bought.

Today, my setup has become more sophisticated. I use Member-Mouse, a Wordpress plugin that lets paying customers into a members only area. Once a new student in my course pays via Stripe or PayPal, they get an automatic email with their login details and can access the course immediately. If someone has trouble with the system, they'll email me, but the current setup is pretty hands-off so I can focus on other parts of my business.

6. How long does it take to create an online class?

It's going to take you longer when you first begin. You just need to get used to your system. Now, I need about four to five hours per day to make a lesson.

First, I research what I'll teach and how I'll structure my class. Researching and writing takes about 90 minutes, then I make my slides in PowerPoint, which takes about 30 minutes. Once you have a system in place for how you want your slides to look, it's just a matter of adding the content. Recording and editing audio takes another 30 minutes, and then you combine the audio with the slides to make a video. I use Windows Movie Maker to do that, and it takes me around ten minutes.

For each lesson, I also prepare practical exercises for my students, so that's another half an hour. And finally, it takes about an hour to set it up on Wordpress and schedule an email to be sent to students.

I'm trying to strike a balance of working five hours a day; three hours in the morning and two hours in the afternoon. I believe five hours is a nice amount of time where you can get enough done and remain focused, but you won't have the feeling you spent the entire day in front of the computer.

7. How do you choose what to teach next?

I sometimes poll my students or I just generally listen to what people say they need. I also have a feedback form at the end of every course. Hearing what your customers think about your work helps you get better.

It's usually not hard to decide *what* to teach; it's more a question of how you'll attract people and make them aware of your course. I would recommend looking for relevant partners and teaming up with others to grow your audience.

> **"TEAM UP WITH OTHERS TO GROW YOUR AUDIENCE."**

8. What resources can you recommend to someone who wants to create an online course?

I've learned a lot from David Siteman Garland, who created The Rise to the Top, and from mynameisbreanne.com. These are two great resources to teach you what you need to know about conversion, promotion, and building an audience if you want to start working in online education.

Many teachers I know don't have a problem creating classes and material, but they have difficulty promoting and selling their work. You need to learn how to market. It's a skill that can be acquired just like any other.

9. What's the biggest challenge for someone who wants to create an online course?

The biggest challenge is to build an audience. It all starts with having visitors to your site opt in to an email list. The list is where you'll generate the majority of your sales. My recommendation is to mention your email list in every piece of content you create and also offer several opt in options throughout your website. When you're ready to launch a course, it's a huge asset to have an audience that already likes your work and wants to learn from you.

There are two ways to grow your list: you can either "publish and hope" people will find you, or you can proactively seek out subscribers. It's a lot easier and faster when you do the latter, especially by collaborating with others. Guest blogging, appearing on podcasts, or doing joint ventures with people with similar audiences can quickly increase the number of your subscribers.

Try to give a lot of value for free or in exchange for people signing up to your e-mail list. Everyone who signs up to mine receives a free e-book with 500 English phrases. Giving something to people that will help them improve their skills is the best thing you can do to build your audience.

One thing to keep in mind about mailing lists is not everyone will open your newsletter. The bigger your audience is, the less people will open your emails. Nowadays, a good mailing list has an open rate of about 25%. People who have smaller lists get up to 50%. You can increase your open rate by sending genuinely useful content and using intriguing subject lines for your messages. Being personable and friendly also goes a long way towards building a relationship with your email subscribers.

10. What's something you would recommend to someone who wants to create an online course?

Once you have an audience, try to get 10-15 paying students to sign up for your first course. If you're insecure about selling, you can invite five to ten people to be beta testers. In other words, give them the course for

free in exchange for their feedback on improving it. Then, you can make the course better and sell it to the rest of your audience more confidently.

Don't hesitate. Make your classes good, but also get them out as quickly as possible. I know people who spend three years working on a course, and I think it's crazy to drag the process out for so long. If you have people wanting to learn from you, you're doing them a disservice by holding back.

Don't be afraid to charge people money for what you're teaching! Your work *is* good enough! If by chance it's not, your students will tell you, and you can always give a refund if someone's dissatisfied.

In a nutshell, build your audience first, then get your first course out there as soon as possible and do it even if you have just five or ten students sign up. Your audience will grow and your content is evergreen, so you can keep selling it for years.

If you're concerned about competition or the large amount of free information available online, remember this – the larger the ocean, the greater the need for a guide to navigate to a destination. When you have people who are interested in your topic and who like your teaching style, that's all you need to build a successful online teaching business.

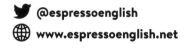

@espressoenglish
www.espressoenglish.net

COLLABORATE WITH OTHERS

I'm going to go ahead and let you in on one of the keys to success. It's a matter of networking. If you know the right people, you gain access to the right places. For centuries, there were hierarchies, but now, since the social web has evolved to what it is today, hierarchies are no longer what they used to be. I would even go as far as saying hierarchies are dead.

Never before has it been easier to gain access to people we don't know who are far away from where we sit in front of our screens. However, in my perception, Twitter has completely revolutionized what's possible and who you can meet for a coffee if you feel like it. Personal websites where people publish their email addresses are like an invitation to write a nice email to whoever you feel deserves a compliment. People are still busy, yet they're accessible.

Creativity is the new currency of social mobility. It's no longer about money or where you've studied; it's what you do (and share online) that makes you stand out to access people and places you might not have even dreamed of. I may be a complete idealist, but I believe we're the generation that makes for what the internet will become in the future. As of now, the internet is younger than 8,000 days, so it's in our hands to make the internet what we want it to be.

To me personally, the internet should be(come) a place where we connect with people to collaborate and learn from each other. The power of networks, the algorithmic ones in terms of how Google works, and why it's important to link to other websites and have others link to yours is what matters if we want to make the social web work in our favor. You can create your own social network and all it takes is linking to the people you admire who might one day link back to you. Be nice, be creative, and tell others why you admire them.

You can collaborate with people actively or passively. If things go well, then passive collaborations can turn into active ones. It's in your hands to make that happen. Wonder how? It, again, starts with you sharing your creative work online.

Once you find your outlet to create out loud, you can use it to compliment other people's work too. You can also use social media to announce what or who you're looking for and people will give you recommendations. Mention brands and companies you want to partner with and people who've inspired you and your work. The more credit you give and the more positive feedback you spread throughout your network, the more visible your work will eventually become.

A passive collaboration is one where the other person doesn't know they're collaborating with you. If you give them credit for having done something that impacted your work, they've collaborated in your process. It feels right to let them know and add to their social, creative currency. If nothing else, it will at least brighten their day to see what they do has an actual impact. You'd appreciate to know when others value your work too, given the effort you put into it to create something of value.

Passive collaborations happen whether you share it with others or not, so why not let the other person know? All it takes is mentioning them on Twitter by quoting their thoughts or a link to their article, or Instagramming a piece of their work and tagging it with their handle or hashtag. Especially successful people spend countless hours working on something, so they should know there are people who appreciate it! Even if you might not think it, the people you deeply admire have bad days just like anyone else. Your post might make all the difference.

Mentioning people online can be the first step to making people you don't personally know (yet) part of your social circle. If you do so repeatedly throughout their career, they'll absolutely notice because there's hardly anyone who has made it. Most people are making it every day!

This is a great moment to pull out your smartphone and tell someone you think their work is awesome! I'll wait...

WRITE AS IF YOU
WOULD BE HAVING
COFFEE WITH A FRIEND.

Now, we've arrived at the sort of collaborations you're probably aware of and recognize as such. Active collaborations are ones that work both ways, and you shouldn't treat them any differently from how you'd treat passive collaborations. Mention the people who have helped you get to where you are today and took work off your shoulders so you could achieve better results. You're in charge of your social success.

Many of the women you've gotten to know in this book, and also the previous book, collaborate with others not just because they enjoy the teamwork, but because it helps them reach audiences beyond their own. If you work together with someone who's on the same mission as you, chances are high their audience might also enjoy your creations. The more people you collaborate with, the more people get exposed to your work along the way.

In a nutshell, admire your allies, passive or active ones. Time for Sarah's story!

Sarah Eichhorn

Sarah is a renowned German lifestyle blogger. When she first started blogging in 2010, she wrote about fashion, but has since broadened her topics to beauty, interior design, and travel.

In her interview, Sarah talks about consistency, transparency, and how to start a blog. In her opinion, having a blog shouldn't be about wanting to become a professional blogger; it's to help you position and grow your business.

📍 **Munich, Germany**

1. What's your educational background and how did you arrive to where you are now?

Since I was 14, I wanted to become a fashion editor. There was a possibility for me to do an internship after I graduated from high school. I had plans to attend college for fashion journalism, but everyone I met during my internship said the college I wanted to go to was a waste of time and money. I didn't know what else to do, so I went on to pursue another internship with a PR agency. I was very lucky because you hardly ever get such an opportunity before you graduate.

Once you have your foot in the door, you have to show people how they can benefit from having you on their team. I don't have a degree, but I would never tell anyone not to study; it worked for me, but that doesn't mean it will work for everyone.

From working in PR, I acquired a lot of incredible contacts and managed to get a position as an assistant to the editor at an online magazine. Eventually, there were some changes in staff and as a consequence, I lost my job. However, I was offered to continue writing for them as a freelancer. About a year later, I started my own blog because I wanted to have a space where I could write about whatever crossed my mind. That was in 2010.

People from the industry knew about me and they also knew I started a blog. Whenever someone from a PR agency or the magazine needed to speak to a blogger, they all thought of me. If you show people what you do, they'll think of you whenever they need someone with your profile. I was one of the first bloggers who got invited to press events. Back then, people didn't know what blogs were and I often had to defend myself being a blogger. I think people only took my blog seriously in 2012, two and a half years after I launched.

> **"IF YOU SHOW PEOPLE WHAT YOU DO, THEY'LL THINK OF YOU WHENEVER THEY NEED SOMEONE WITH YOUR PROFILE."**

2. How did you find your first clients?

Even though I didn't work for other companies for more than two and a half years before I went freelance, I managed to build a network while I had my full-time job. Once I was available for hire as a freelancer, I reached out to the people I knew might be interested in my services. I sent them emails with references and I included a motivational letter. It was just like any normal application, but with the exception that I wasn't available for full-time employment. Because I run an online business, I didn't meet my clients in person for a really long time. Now I know all of them in person, but at the beginning we only communicated via email or Skype.

Due to my references I acquired from the magazine, I had a strong profile and started working with several leading outlets. I also have two brands for whom I create articles for their blog and I write for multiple magazines. If you don't have any references, start writing for yourself to have something to show.

3. What are your different income streams?

I have my blog, which is my biggest income source. I publish advertorials, I feature ads, and I earn money through affiliate links. I also have a store on my blog, so every time someone buys something through my blog, I'll make commission. I then have some clients I write for every month and sometimes, I get booked to cover a story for a magazine or a brand. I'm no longer just booked as a freelance fashion writer; it's mostly because I have the perspective of a fashion blogger.

The shop that's connected to my website features items I've bought myself. When you have a blog, people come because they like your taste, so you should only show pieces that feel authentic. I implemented Trac-Delight, the performance network for fashion, to my blog shortly after it was launched. I like the idea of curating my own store. I think people who come to a blog for inspiration appreciate knowing where to purchase what they see.

I generally only work with clients that feel right because it makes no sense taking on jobs you know don't excite you. If you're not fully convinced, then your audience won't be either. Your readers trust you and your judgement, so you can't disappoint them. When you have a blog, you can't just accept pitches and write about the things people pay you for. It's important to offer a lot of editorial content you haven't been paid to produce. I have a set number of advertorials I accept per month. I believe you need to write at least twice as much unpaid content as what you get paid to write and publish. Don't overdo it with ads!

"IF YOU'RE NOT FULLY CONVINCED, DON'T BLOG ABOUT IT."

The advertorials I feature on my blog are either image series, articles, or photo shootings I produce together with the brands. I really like the diversity of my job; sometimes I'm home for weeks and then I get to go to a Fashion Week or some other event.

The concept of my blog is to show the pretty sights of life, which, of course, gives me a lot of creative freedom. My blog is interesting to brands because I showcase what young, modern women are interested in, and those young, modern women are interested in having someone select relevant items specifically for them. Sometimes I'll post an expensive handbag I treated myself to, and other times I'll share the bargain I scavenged at a sale. Reading my blog is like having a cup of coffee with an old friend.

"DON'T TRADE YOUR TIME FOR MONEY."

From a business perspective, I think it's important to have multiple income streams and earn money without trading your time. In 2014, my husband and I went on a trip around the world for 13 months and I remained working with my clients, even though I wasn't in Germany. I consider myself very fortunate for having a profession where I can be wherever I want to be and remain working with the people I do. I've always blogged when we went on vacation, so I knew what I was getting into. Sometimes it was difficult to find good internet, so when we arrived in a new country, I always bought a sim card first to make sure I could at least tether if there was no other way to go online. That's the downside of an online business; you must be reachable 24/7.

4. How do you deal with the business side of having a blog now?

There was no business model when I started my blog. No one back then had one. A blog was a place for me to share what I was interested in and it helped get people interested in working with me. I work with an agency now; all the advertorials and ads are organized and booked by them.

At the beginning of 2013, the founder of the agency I'm represented by approached me about their plans. I loved the idea and because I trusted and admired them for their work, I immediately signed up. It was a time when bloggers in other countries already had agents, so I felt honored they thought of me. At first, the agency signed with six bloggers, but now they represent more than 30 bloggers from Germany.

The team that represents me knows what I like, so they only send me requests they know will fit my style. I no longer have to go through every single email myself. I only get a selection of emails that are relevant to me, which saves an immense amount of time. I also don't have to negotiate with clients anymore. Agencies make sure bloggers get the best deal, which makes it worth it that they take a cut from the earnings.

5. What does your creative process look like?

Sometimes, I see a picture I like and I think of a text to go with it, or I might already have an idea in my head and slowly fumble to a finished thought. Sometimes, I can write a text within 30 minutes, or other times, it takes much longer because I always try to come up with a story. Some articles are written weeks in advance, and others just 30 minutes before I hit "publish."

On my blog, I've initiated theme days, so now that I know what the overall theme is, it's just about finding topics that fit. Categories help me make sure all my readers get what they're interested in the most and that the allocation of topics I cover is equal. My blog wouldn't be what it is without my readers, so that's my main focus when planning what to write. I like to do series on my blog and whenever I want to do a new one, I ask my audience what they would enjoy. I give my readers a couple of options I'm interested in myself because it makes no sense to write about something my readers don't enjoy. They're why I can do what I do.

I decided to have theme days after I came back from my trip around the world. During the time on the road, I mostly blogged about travel. I didn't want go back into covering fashion exclusively and I knew I wanted to continue writing about travel. Because my husband and I were moving into a new apartment, I wanted to explore interior design and write about that too. Now, I write a weekly summary every Monday, I dedicate an article to travel on Tuesdays, I post an outfit on Wednesdays, Thursdays are to show my interior inspiration, Fridays are dedicated to beauty, Saturdays are a surprise day where I post anything I'm enjoying in that moment, and I post another outfit of the day on Sundays.

My days aren't necessarily structured. The only constant is a to-do list I work through each day. I kick off each month with a list of what I want to accomplish and then I break it down. Of course, something unexpected may happen and the list changes and grows as the month progresses, but that's how I try to keep my business structured.

6. How do new readers find your blog?

A lot of my readers have been my readers since the very beginning. Five years ago, I wrote about different topics than I do now. Over the years, my audience has, just like myself, gotten older and changed, so the readers who enjoy my blog enjoy it because they have similar taste. I might've lost people who only came to read what I had to say about fashion, but I don't want to slave away and stop evolving, so it's okay to let readers go as long as new readers come along.

A lot of people find me on Google. Having blogged regularly for so many years increases your Google ranking. Being consistent and publishing new content regularly is important when you want your readers come back for more.

What I think is also very important is when other people link to your blog. Meeting other bloggers and mentioning them in your articles is crucial to help them grow their community, as it also helps you grow yours. In the earlier days, many bloggers used to have a blogroll where they would feature blogs they liked, and it's upsetting to me that it's no longer the case because so many bloggers see one another as competitors.

I post teasers of my blog articles to Instagram and Facebook. I use IFTTT to repost from Facebook to Twitter and sometimes, I pay for Facebook ads if something is important to me and I want people to see it.

7. What's your long-term vision for your blog?

From the beginning, blogs were meant to change the perception of what's fashionable. For a very long time, the fashion industry has propagated extremely thin women. I would like to change the perception of what's understood as fashionable. Of course, I can't do that by myself, but I can at least try. The first wave of fashion bloggers were all trying to democratize what fashion is, so it feels a little contradictory that bloggers now all look like models; it's unrealistic. I really want to see size 38 or 40, the normal women, be accepted as pretty. It can't be true that we only support girls who starve to be size 34 or 36 for a little bit of online glamour. I really believe every type of feminine body is beautiful and deserves to be treated as such.

8. What's something you would recommend to someone who wants to start a blog?

I personally use Wordpress to host my blog because there are so many different themes you can install to make your blog stand out. I work with a web developer who helps me with the technical side of things, and I have a designer who makes it look pretty. My husband takes all my pictures. You need someone you trust because being photographed is highly personal, especially if the photos are being published.

I've learned a lot about blogging while working for an online magazine. Some of the mistakes many people make is they steal images they find on Google. You can get fined for using images you don't own the rights for, so always make it your business to reach out to the owners of the images you'd like to use.

Find a niche and create a concept before you start. I don't think you can just post whatever comes to mind if you want to have success. You need to put the reader at the center of your focus. When you think about the topic you want to write about, it should be something you see your-self exploring for years to come. It shouldn't be a topic you'll be through with after writing three posts. Also, think about how often you want to publish articles and how often it's possible for you to do so. Some people start with such incredible enthusiasm and then stop after only a couple of weeks because they don't have enough time to write.

Make sure to either learn how to take beautiful pictures or look for a source of good imagery. Bloggers have really professionalized their visu-al content. You can't just upload a mediocre picture you took with your phone. Make sure your blog is visually appealing.

Then, once you decide on a nice template for your blog, get your own domain name. It's worth the €15 a year if you want to be taken se-riously. And last but not least, make sure you use correct grammar. If English isn't your mother tongue but you want to write in English, get someone to proofread your work. If you know you struggle with gram-mar in your mother tongue too, find someone to help you get that part right.

9. How do you spread the word about your blog?

I'm on all social media channels because that's an important compo-nent of my profession. I post consistently to every single one of them. I believe a blog should help you spread the word about your business. It's a great channel for you to show your unique perspective and if you talk to someone, they'll probably check you out online. Having a blog will help them recognize what you're good at. See your blog as your business card, but don't aim at making your blog your profession from day one because that probably won't work.

10. What are the biggest challenges for someone who wants to blog professionally?

It's a lot of work, far more than what it seems from the outside. You've got to do a lot of research and answer tons of emails, and you also have to be available 24/7. Many people only see the glamorous side of being a blogger; all the events you get invited to and all the pretty dresses you receive for free, but people tempt to forget you have to go home and edit

**SEE YOUR BLOG AS
YOUR BUSINESS CARD.**

images to publish an article first thing in the morning. You also have to invest in your blog before you see any return, and proactively approach companies and agencies to work with you. When I first started, it took years. It's quicker now, but you must be professional to keep up with the amount of bloggers out there. To be respected, you must be able to deliver numbers that are relevant to the companies you want to win as your partners. You need to create a media kit for your site where you explain your profile and describe what type of readers visit your blog. And you need to make your numbers public; how many people visit your blog monthly, how long they surf through your site. You need to make yourself accountable.

When you join the blogger world, no one's waiting for you, so you have to remain persistent and keep blogging regularly. I think it would make so much more sense for professionals to blog about their journey and what it takes to do their job. There's space for professionals to help grow their businesses through content marketing, but I'm not sure how much space there is for full-time bloggers. Nevertheless, anything's possible if you've got a good concept!

"ANYTHING'S POSSIBLE IF YOU'VE GOT A GOOD CONCEPT!"

@josieloves
www.josieloves.de

EXPLORE ALL POSSIBILITIES

The possibilities of what you can do with your creative output are endless. Your art and your thoughts aren't solid rock. Instead, your visions are fluid, expandable, and translatable into other forms of output.

When I first talked to Joanna (you'll read about her in the next chapter), she said she doesn't just write books. They're not her actual products. A book is just one of her mediums to reach people to whom her work matters. It's her thoughts that are of value that she can translate into different forms. In her opinion, Joanna would never reach everyone who may enjoy her stories if she only published them as books. As she puts it, not all of us read, which is unfortunate, but true.

Just because not everyone consumes ideas and thoughts in one way doesn't mean we shouldn't look for other ways to reach those we think might appreciate our creations. Getting back to Joanna's example, she realized some people prefer to enjoy her stories by listening to them, which translates into even more possibilities to make a living with her creative work. She's created podcasts, audiobooks, and tutorials, and if you thought this is all, Joanna also gives talks at events and conferences.

It's not the coffee mug that has your print on it that gets people excited; it's the print that's on the coffee mug. It's your style that delights people you should build upon, and there are millions of ways to make the most out of your unique approach to life and work.

The possibilities of how far you can go with your creativity depends on those you serve with your work; what are the habits of the people you serve that you can cater to? What more can you do to solve their problems and how can you deliver something to make their lives easier, more beautiful, and more enjoyable? By looking at the needs, habits, and desires of others, you'll discover what you can create to benefit them.

The catch? People have different habits. They might love your style, but it's just the form in which you share your work, or the product you have chosen to produce, that doesn't necessarily fit their lifestyles. Some people don't have time to read, but they spend hours commuting to work and need something to entertain them. Others might not need the font you've created, but they like it and wish to buy an art piece for their apartment featuring a quote written in your font. It doesn't really matter what your final product has been to this day because there are so many possibilities to what you can do out of what you've been doing to fulfill differing desires.

A very lucky coincidence happened about a week after I interviewed Joanna for this book. The lovely Abigail Besdin from Skillshare reached out to me asking if I was interested in hosting a class on their platform. I immediately agreed for two reasons: after I taped the video for my first Kickstarter campaign, I swore to myself I'd tape myself more often this year (I blame the fact we taped it on New Year's Eve that I made such a crazy resolution). The other reason was because of what Joanna told me; I wanted to see if she was right about being able to use something you've already created in multiple ways. Together with Nataleigh Kohn, I created and adapted the outline of the content of *This Year Will Be Different* and packaged it as an online tutorial. Some of the people who liked my Skillshare class also bought my book (thank you), and even though a lot of the content was what they had already heard, they still got value from reading the book because they had the chance to highlight important notes and read the insightful interviews I didn't share on Skillshare.

It might take time until you figure out ways to create new and additional products. You might also need to source the right partners to do that, given your time is limited. However, you should schedule a slot in your calendar to reflect and research new possibilities of how you can create additional income streams.

I've mentioned her enough, so now it's time to finally hear Joanna's story yourself!

Joanna Penn

Joanna is a self-published author who splits her time between writing fiction and nonfiction that helps other writers market their books. She began self-publishing in 2007, before Amazon invented the Kindle.

In her interview, Joanna explains what it takes to go from just having an idea to marketing one. She also touches on how you shouldn't think of a book as one product, but rather as a platform for multiple income streams.

⊙ **London, UK**

1. What's your educational background and how did you arrive to where you are now?

Originally, I wanted to help bring peace back to the Middle East, so I studied theology. However, after graduation, I became a management consultant. Later on, I studied psychology and received my masters. I haven't studied English or how to write, but I use a lot of what I learned in university when writing fiction.

I worked in consulting for 13 years. It was probably how it is for many people after university; you get your first job and you don't really think about what you do. You go to work, you pay your bills, and suddenly you wake up one day and you feel disconnected.

In my twenties, there was a lot of pressure about how your life is supposed to be; you were supposed to have a particular job, have a mortgage, and everything else that's meant to impress people. And I did: I had a high-paying job that made me miserable!

In 2000, I decided to quit and moved across the world. I went to Australia first, and then to New Zealand where I started a scuba diving business, a business that ultimately failed. Afterwards, I went into property investment, which worked out about the same as the scuba diving business. I decided to go back into consulting, but also wrote a self-help book. I wanted to write it mostly for myself to get me out of my situation and discover what I really wanted to do with my life.

I sacrificed money for time and cut down to a four-day week. I believe if you want to change something about your life, you need to clear a space for the new you. For me, the new me was to become a writer. So, I started writing.

> **"IF YOU WANT TO CHANGE SOMETHING ABOUT YOUR LIFE, CLEAR A SPACE IN YOUR SCHEDULE FOR THE NEW YOU."**

Writing that book literally changed my life. I don't know how many other lives the book changed, but they say the first book you write is the one you *have* to write.

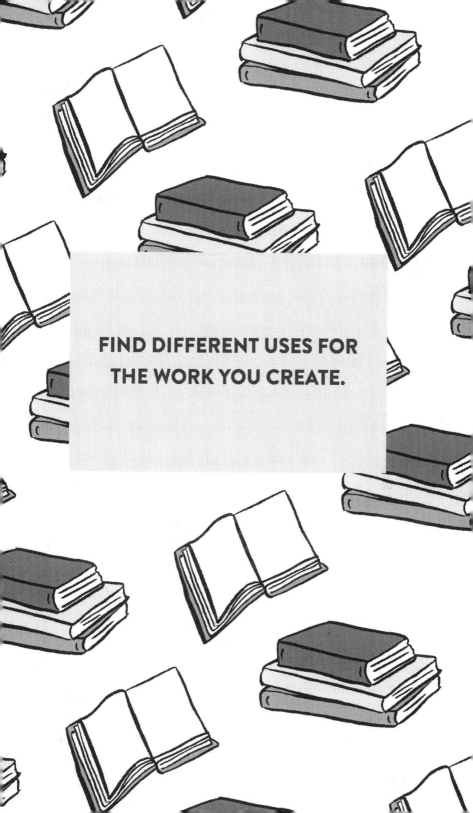

**FIND DIFFERENT USES FOR
THE WORK YOU CREATE.**

I didn't know anything about the publishing industry at that point, so once I finished writing, I began researching the marketing side of publishing. That was in 2007 when there was no Kindle and no affordable print on demand option. Almost everyone who published books did so the traditional way, so I happened to get into self-publishing before it became a thing. I just didn't want to wait, as is common in traditional publishing.

In 2008, I started *The Creative Penn* and began writing more books. It took a year before anyone noticed my blog, and over a year to get to 1,000 followers on Twitter. It also took three years for me to write three novels and only then did my book-related income seem like a way to build a prosperous business. Writing books is not a "get rich quickly" scheme.

I wrote my first four books and built my blog while working full-time. I used to get up at 5am and write for an hour before work. In 2011, I was able to leave my day job and fully focus on building my career as a writer. It's really important to schedule time you don't usually have to be able to grow, and then to eventually maybe leave your job.

2. What are your different income streams?

I'm an author-entrepreneur. All my income stems from my writing, but I separate that into books and blogs, since the latter brings me speaking opportunities and affiliate income as well as direct sales. In 2015, I reached a six-figure income, which half was generated through book sales; 60% was generated through my fiction literature and 40% through my guides for authors. So despite what the media says, it is possible to make a full-time living as a self-published author.

The other half of my income breaks down to courses I made and sell through my website. Then, I also make an income through affiliate links, professional speaking, and sponsorship for my podcast.

I believe in multiple income streams. You might think of your book as one product, but what you really have is the potential to make money on different platforms, and in different countries, by translating the content to different mediums, such as paperbacks, e-books, audiobooks, and podcasts. Remember this whenever someone offers you a book contract! If you decide to go the traditional route, make sure you only sell rights to what the publishing house is willing to exploit for you, like different countries, languages, and forms, i.e. e-books, print, or audio. Don't sell the rights to what they won't use because then you can self-publish where they don't and make an extra income.

I also don't rely on Amazon exclusively. I'm on Kobo, iBook, Nook, and all the other platforms to have my income streams as widely spread as possible. Should any of the platforms I use change their terms of use, I'll be okay because I've built other streams over time. As a creative, it's important to build as many pillars for your business as possible. If you're easily overwhelmed by unnecessary bureaucracy and the amount of platforms available to you, use Trackerbox by StoryBoxSoftware to see all of your income streams in one place.

"BUILD AS MANY PILLARS FOR YOUR BUSINESS AS POSSIBLE. BE CREATIVE!"

I got laid off during the global financial crisis and that's when I realized relying on one business to support you might not be such a smart option. As a freelancer, you can build several income streams, which will make for a stable business.

3. How does self-publishing work?

In the earlier days, a lot of professional speakers used to self-publish because they could sell books out of the backroom. Even today, many speakers and consultants write books not because they want to make a profit, but because they can monetize the "back-end" of the books. Books for nonfiction authors act more as a business card, as well as providing status and qualified leads for the author. Nonfiction books often don't need to make money; it's the other services you make available that are more important for the cash flow. Which, of course, doesn't mean they don't make money because they do!

It used to be very expensive to self-publish. You had to do a print run and you had to keep the books in your house until you sold out. So when Amazon invented the Kindle, that completely revolutionized the entire industry! It gave everyone who wanted to publish the possibility to do so. The barrier of entry to self-publishing is now the cost of a professional editor and a professional cover designer.

Being a self-published writer means you have the freedom to publish however and wherever you want. I've sold books in more than 68 countries. When you're with a publishing house, you don't know whether they will distribute your book to so many countries. I believe that as a self-published writer, you can make more money with less sales. On Kindle, even if you sell your book for just $2.99, you'll still make $2 profit. Traditionally, published authors make much less than that. They're also tied to their contracts and what the publishing house decides to do with their book. For traditional publishing, the risk is that you give too much away, and for self-publishing, the risk is that you don't make your money back. Some authors started using crowdfunding platforms to pay the upfront costs.

Since Amazon bought CreateSpace, it's very affordable for self-published writers to sell print. With CreateSpace, the author doesn't have to do any of the necessary logistics because Amazon will print and distribute to the readers directly. You'll just receive the royalties. It's very convenient. Then, the other great opportunity for self-publishers is the possibility to sell their books as audio. The good thing about audio is people can multitask while listening to your audiobook. ACX.com might be available in just a few countries at the moment, but I'm sure that will change.

When you think about self-publishing and that the margins for self-published writers are at 70%, it seems odd to publish any other way. However, you'll need to consider the tax implications of earning royalties in your country. If you're a non-US citizen earning money through Amazon, Smashwords, or other US companies, you need to follow the tax rule. If you don't fill in your W8-BEN, you will have 30% tax withheld and your books may even be withdrawn from sale. As a US citizen, you'll need to register with your tax number in order to receive royalties; otherwise, Amazon will withhold your tax amount. I don't give legal advice, but if you want to learn more about earning money with US companies, a great resource is bit.ly/USincometax.

3. How did you self-publish your first book?

My first book wasn't available online, so today, I would do a lot different-ly because we now have tools that enable us to reach a much wider au-dience. I sold my first book whenever I spoke at events. I must have sold only about 200 copies. Selling books like that was very hard because I'm an introvert. Even today, a lot of things continue to challenge my comfort zone, but with the internet, a lot has changed, especially when people started buying online. I've sold nearly half a million books now because everything you do online helps grow your audience.

The most important learning for me is that one book is never going to be enough. Occasionally, there will be a lightning strike and someone will make money from having written just one book, but generally, you need to write a series of books to make an income. It's a very gradual cal-culation; the more books you write and the more virtual shelf space you occupy for yourself, the easier it will be for people to discover you and the more money you will make. When you have one book, you might sell 100 a year, but when you have three books, you might sell 100,000 a year because it will be easier for people to discover your books. Also, the more you write, the better you'll get at writing. I was guilty of trying to hype my first novel because it took so long and I thought it was as precious as a snowflake. I still believe you have to hustle those first thou-sand sales with everything you have, but my income and sales jumped when I released the second novel with very little fanfare because I al-ready had an established presence on Amazon.

"ONE BOOK MAKES YOU A WRITER. SEVERAL BOOKS MAKE YOU AN AUTHOR-ENTREPRENEUR."

I've published more than 15 books: five nonfiction guides and ten fiction books, and that's why I'm making a decent income. It's like with any oth-er job. When you start working, how much are you worth in your first year? You do an internship and earn close to nothing! Then, after three years, you earn a little more and then in your tenth year, you've become really valuable and suddenly earn a lot! The same goes for books. The more you have in your backlog, the more money you can make. Just like with any career, it takes time to build up.

4. What does your creative process look like?

I get ideas everywhere, just like any other creative! I have an app on my phone called Things where I capture ideas that cross my mind. I also keep notebooks. I'm constantly writing down learnings and things that come to me, and when I'm ready to start writing an actual book, I decide on the title and the broad topic.

The first time I decided to write a fiction book was in 2009. I participated in the #NaNoWriMo program and wrote a 50,000 novel in 30 days. I never used any of the material, but it made me realize I could actually write fiction.

To give you an example, the idea for my latest book, *Deviance*, is based on a story I learned about when researching. I discovered that in Southwark, London, the church once licensed brothels. That sounded really interesting to me and made me think I was onto something.

I write fiction to explore themes that interest me in places that fascinate me with characters I would like to read about. And I write nonfiction in order to understand what I want to learn for myself. When I think about nonfiction books I want to write, they're aimed at people like me, so I know the problems my readers have. They're my problems too. I wrote *Career Change* because I wanted to change careers. I wrote *Business for Authors* because I needed to codify what I thought about being a writer and running a business. Writing helps me think.

Whenever I write, I use Scrivener. With nonfiction books, I first specify the table of contents and then fill in the blanks. With fiction, I plan a one-pager with a few scenes. I know where I want the book to begin and how I want the book to end, and then I go to a local café around the corner and write nonstop until I have a first draft.

Whenever I work on a book, I spend about a month writing every morning for a couple of hours. When I have a first draft, I print it out and edit it by hand. You have to understand the first draft is really just the barebones of a finished work. And that it's probably crap.

MAKE TIME FOR WRITING.
PUT IT IN YOUR DIARY.

During my editing process, I write all kinds of notes in the margins, scribble, and cross things out. For fiction, I jot down new scenes that need writing, continuity issues, problems with characters, and much more. That first pass usually takes a while. Then, I implement my changes in Scrivener, print the manuscript again, and edit it at least one more time before I send it to my editor. I have an editor for fiction and a different one for nonfiction. If you're planning to write your first book, you should consider getting a structural editor too. You'll learn a lot.

Once I get the manuscript back, I add the changes and send it to my beta readers. I prefer to have a group of five or six readers because they'll give me six different opinions from a reader's perspective. My main rule with beta readers is I only make changes if more than one person says the same thing. Then, I'll send it to a proofreader.

The first time you receive a line edit, it hurts. You think you're a great writer and then someone changes practically every word. I know my editing process is rather extensive, but I believe editing makes a book stronger. That's also why I believe professional editing is non-negotiable for serious career writers such as yourself!

I also work with a professional cover designer and a layout designer for the interior of my print books. For e-books, I do the formatting myself.

5. How does your process look once you've published a book?

I use a Filofax calendar and have the next three to six months mapped out. I also have a word count calendar on the wall with my daily achievements, and I use the OfficeTime app on my iPhone to track the hours I spent creating or doing all of the administrative work. I tempt to alternate between writing fiction and nonfiction. I write in my calendar when I'm going to start working on the next novel. Writing is what I do for a living, and I treat it seriously. It's in my diary.

> **"WHEN YOU WANT TO WRITE FOR A**
> **LIVING, INCLUDE IT IN YOUR DIARY."**

I always keep journals; I write notes and do research, but I also have a cycle for when I publish. Now, in my tenth year, I only need to announce a new book to my mailing list. I've been building my mailing list for years, so now if I send out an email, I can push my new book to the bestseller list just because of that. Every author needs to build a mailing list!

When you start out, it's very difficult to market your books because you don't have enough reviews. I have a group of readers who get early access and review my book on the first day or in the first week. Then, because I publish series of books, I usually do a paid promotion and give away the first book for free.

I believe what's more important than an impressive launch is the ability to establish good monthly sales over time. You'll feel better if your income just keeps ticking in. The launch approach comes from the traditional book publishing world because they only have a small window when they can focus on marketing your book before moving onto the next one. I believe the world of books has changed and it's becoming more about establishing continuous sales. A book is always new to the reader who has just found it, so you don't need to worry too much about launching properly.

What also helps is looking at yourself and thinking about how you personally find new books. Sometimes, people find books because they browse through a bookstore and a cover catches their eye. Or, they browse a category they are interested in online, look through a reader community, such as Goodreads, or they have a specific question and search for books that can give them what they are looking for. For example, "I need a business plan." Also, many people find books because someone they trust recommends one to them. Amazon also sends an email with books you might be interested in, or when an author you bought a book from in the past published a new one.

People also might have heard an interview with you as an author. They found a set you've created about a specific topic on Pinterest, they read an article you wrote online, or they met you at a networking event and liked what you do. Then, they might sign up to your mailing list and enjoy what you share, and once you publish another book, they might be amongst the first who buy. So don't waste your energy on making a huge launch event. Instead, focus on continuous marketing tactics, like building your mailing list.

6. How did you build your mailing list?

Everything you do platform-wise should be about trying to drive people to your email list so you can contact them again.

Nonfiction authors can grow their links with blogging, podcasting, Youtube, Pinterest, and so on. There are so many possibilities! As long as there is a clickable link to your book sales page or a signup form to your mailing list, it's good marketing. I was once on national TV and didn't sell a single book after that. Your marketing efforts should make it as easy as possible for people to buy your books. Marketing nowadays really is every author's job! However, it's different for fiction because readers shop in the bookstores directly, so you need a number of books. You'll need to make one permanently free to drive people to your circle. It's very different marketing fiction from marketing nonfiction. However, it's advisable to mention your mailing list in all kinds of books.

Six years ago, I created a blueprint for writers and that has been bringing people to my mailing list ever since. That list is the engine to my nonfiction book sales because people who are interested in that topic will subscribe to the list and eventually buy.

Then with fiction, I always have at least one book available for free to get people on my mailing list when they visit my website. I use the mailing list to tell people whenever a book is available.

The mailing list approach works much better for nonfiction than fiction. With fiction, it's much harder to figure out who you're targeting.

7. What's something you would like to recommend to people who want to self-publish?

Allow for your first draft to be crap. Set yourself goals for how many words you want to write a day. Stephen King aims at writing 2,000 words, if this helps give you an idea. If you don't have some kind of a goal, you won't achieve anything.

8. What resources would you recommend to someone who wants to start publishing?

Because so many people ask me about this, I started publishing books and podcasts to help people become writers. Everyone who signs up to my mailing list gets access to the *Author 2.0 Blueprint*. I would also recommend Scrivener or Write or Die to help you get writing and Freedom or Anti-Social to get undistracted chunks of time for you to focus.

9. What are the greatest challenges for someone who wants to become a self-published author?

It's expensive to publish your first book. You'll also have to learn how to write a whole book. It's hard, even for people who have been reading all their lives. Once you go through all of that, you realize that not many people care about your work, which is why, after you've learned about writing, you'll need to learn about marketing.

Also, you may realize at this point that the first draft isn't the finished book. Many people assume that the book they pick up at the store just came out like that from the writer's pen, so when they're trying to write a book themselves, they think they're awful writers. As a writer, you need to learn to self-edit your work. The first draft is hardly ever exceptionally good. It's hard work and you'll need to reread your own work many times.

The other challenge is you need to learn to manage your time wisely when you want to become a professional writer. You need to also manage all your creative hats, as well as your business hats. Don't mix up writing time with marketing time; you should always separate them. However, you still need to schedule both!

> **"IF YOU DON'T HAVE SOME KIND OF A GOAL, YOU WON'T ACHIEVE ANYTHING."**

10. What practical steps would you recommend to a first time author?

First, finalize your manuscript. I've had so many people ask me about publishing before they even started writing a manuscript. Writing is incredibly difficult, so before you start thinking about doing anything else, write! Check out #NaNoWriMo and if your timing isn't anywhere close to November, do a #NaNoWriMo just for yourself or together with a friend.

Once you have a self-edited manuscript, look for a team to help you be a real, professional writer. An editor and a professional cover designer are a must! And not just for print, but also for e-books.

Once you have that sorted, get your own URL and look for someone who can help you build a website. This is also a good moment to write your author's bio and a blurb for the back of your book and for Amazon.

Finally, it's time for you to publish. If you're new to writing, you might want to explore the available ways to promote your book. For new authors, I would recommend joining the KDP select program for the initial 90 days to get some traction with a free giveaway. You need to also think about how you will price your book to remain competitive. If the majority of e-books sell for less than $9.99 and a lot of fiction is under $7.99, then you can't charge more if you're a first time author. And if you want to see your book in print, try CreateSpace. You'll feel great once you hold your book in your hands!

Next, it's time to think about marketing your book. My initial suggestions would be to use some kind of promo pricing or KDP select. Set up your author profile on Amazon's Author Central and add your book in multiple formats on Goodreads.

Get business cards with the cover of your book on them. I can recommend moo.com, but there are other services too. Business cards will come in handy at networking events.

Don't forget to pick a social media platform, one you're already using, and start sharing more about your book. Tell stories. And most importantly of all, start writing your *next* book!

🐦 @thecreativepenn
🌐 www.thecreativepenn.com

BUILD MULTIPLE INCOME STREAMS

This probably doesn't come as a newsflash, but when you start out as a freelancer, you don't already have multiple income streams; you most likely start out with one. In the early stages of freelancing, it's very likely you will start with, what I described in *This Year Will Be Different*, a lot of insecurities and a long to-do list of things you need to accomplish to position yourself in the world of creative freelancers. However, building multiple income streams is something you should aspire to do and start pursuing as early as possible, which, as far as I'm concerned, might be exactly...today!

All the ladies you've met throughout this book have shared their different income streams that support their businesses. Hearing how they put their creativity to use in different ways made me realize how fortunate I was for being able to ask this question. I believe it's important to spark a discussion about why and how to invest your time and efforts into opening up different sources of income to support yourself. I don't recall ever asking any of my friends directly about this, and thus, I feel like you owe your other freelance and employed friends this favor. You should confront them next time you meet up for a coffee ask, "What do you do to support yourself when things don't go as planned?"

When I worked for a company, I thought I had a stable job. It's the vision that's being sold to us that having a job in a company is the more secure life choice. However, only after I got fired from my first job after graduating from university, I finally realized I was fully dependent on the mercy and mood swings of someone who hardly knew who I was.

Suddenly, having just one source of income didn't feel safe to me at all anymore.

Whether you're self-employed or work for a company, you should make the effort to think about other ways to generate an income. The more diverse your portfolio of income streams is, the better you'll sleep at night knowing that if anything happens, there will be at least some sort of an income arriving in your bank account every month.

Being as talented a person as you are, it's utterly up to you to think of some different activities to pursue to make some extra cash. Having access to the social web gives you the tools to create something that's scalable and can be distributed multiple times to others while remaining equally beneficial. Think of what Joanna said about digital products, or wait for what you'll hear from Patty. Reminding yourself of Sara's story at this point makes sense too, when you think of her extra income stream being the Joshua Tree House.

Given you're labeled as a creative, you have the freedom to experiment with different techniques and outlets and do whatever you desire that will add value to others. I've mentioned previously that I sell my photographs on EyeEm, even though I'm not a photographer, so give yourself the freedom to try things out that you're curious about. If you're not sure what you could produce, think about what you know and could teach others that could make for an extra income once you upload it to an e-learning platform of your liking, such as Skillshare, Udemy, or Lynda.

Once you settle on what you want to try out and play with, pursuing that activity should become one of your weekly rituals. You've already heard about the importance of the quantity of qualitative content from Susan, and you also remember how Joanna emphasized on the importance of occupying more digital shelf space with your work. Building viable income streams won't happen overnight, but starting to think about different options will make you more open and switched on to start looking for new ways that could eventually stabilize your business.

At the beginning, this side income might buy you a beer, then later on, maybe a dinner. However, if you pursue this path and keep adding to your bucket of marketable content, this source of income could become

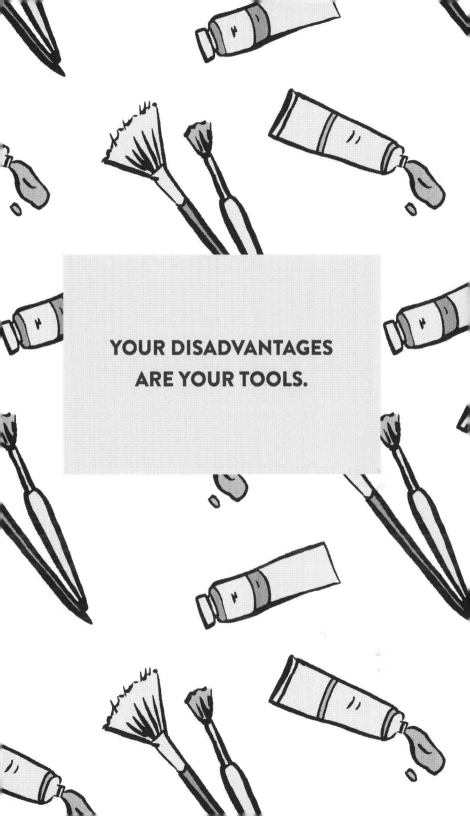

YOUR DISADVANTAGES
ARE YOUR TOOLS.

significant enough to free up some of your time to experiment with your creativity even more.

The majority of people I've spoken with about how they started their businesses have grown them organically from an interest or hobby they pursued next to their regular jobs. Their side hustle suddenly earned them more than their full-time jobs, so they were able to quit. Vicky Heiler, the founder of the blog *Bikini & Passport*, whose story you might've read in my first book, was such a case. Her blog became so successful, she could make a living as a full-time fashion blogger. She's by far not an exception, if you consider how it all started for Susan, who you've met earlier in this book. So while you should explore what different possibilities could eventually become a major source of your monthly income, it might be something you didn't even think would work out that way at all.

Some of your unique talents might be skills you underestimate. Jaymay, whose music you might know if you were a fan of *How I Met Your Mother*, never thought making art could ever be something that would support her. If you don't share your creative work with others, you'll never know if you have a chance of turning it into something of monetary value.

Once again, when you find yourself at the crossroads of deciding whether to share your art versus keeping it in a drawer, you should remind yourself you don't have anything to lose if you try. It's not a risk; it's a chance because what can go wrong? If you're insecure about something not helping your personal brand become more outstanding, you can always publish your work under a fake name until you feel comfortable enough to admit the work is yours. If you add value to people and if you work with the right partners, this can be a way to go from being a freelancer to being a creative entrepreneur, and as a creative entrepreneur, you'll be able to proudly say your art feeds you. And maybe your family. Think about it.

In the meantime, it's time for another interview: Jaymay's. I'd recommend looking for her music on Spotify. She's one of those "feel good" musicians. Happy listening and reading!

Jamie Seerman

aka Jaymay

Jaymay is a singer-songwriter and artist who found her calling during an open mic night in New York City. In her opinion, your disadvantages are your tools.

In her interview, Jaymay sheds light on how to make money as a musician and how to channel your creativity to make it work to your advantage.

📍 **Los Angeles, USA**

1. What's your educational background and how did you arrive to where you are now?

When I was looking at colleges, I wanted to find one where I would be able to design my own curriculum. I wanted to travel and, perhaps, study abroad for a while. My mom brought my attention to New College in Sarasota, Florida, which is where I ended up. It's a really small, unconventional school. I studied in Florence, Italy and New York City as well.

I've always been self-motivated and creative. I wasn't interested in multiple choice testing. I could never imagine a future working in an office behind a desk, but that I would ultimately become a musician was totally unexpected.

I've always loved music. We had two broken (or just very out of tune) pianos in our house, and I learned to play the violin in third grade when everyone was required to choose an instrument. I bought a guitar when I was 18 and wrote during my entire college education. I would perform covers around campus and get together with other musicians. I rarely shared my original songs and when I did, they weren't performed with much confidence.

During my sophomore year, a friend introduced me to an open mic at a bar, The Sidewalk Cafe, located at 6th Street and Avenue A in NYC. I watched in awe as she sang for the crowd and swore to myself I would one day return and attempt the same. Upon graduating, I moved in with my sister on the Upper East Side and began attending that same open mic every Monday night. The first time I performed, I had this special feeling; I just knew it was what I wanted to do forever.

Of course, to pay my share of the rent, I had to find a job, so I became an office manager at an Italian restaurant about an hour outside the city. I remember having to take the subway, metro-north railroad, and a bus or taxi to get there. I was late on my first day because I stayed at the open mic till 4am the previous night. I lasted two months as the office manager and then babysat to pay the bills.

2. How did you go from having all these odd jobs to becoming a professional musician?

That first open mic performance in 2003 marked the beginning of my career. From there, I was offered gigs at bigger venues where a tip jar was passed around to collect money. I kept writing, rehearsing (sometimes with a band), performing, and building my name.

In 2005, I got together with bass player, Jared Engel, and we recorded an EP in my bedroom in Brooklyn. Without money to pay for a studio or a producer, we had no option but to teach ourselves pro-tools, and we mostly recorded every instrument on the same mic. I named the EP "Sea Green, See Blue" and shared it on every available digital platform. A company called A to Z Media printed my CDs, which I sold at all my shows. I painted the album artwork myself.

Through word-of-mouth and internet exposure, exciting things started happening. iTunes called me out of the blue and said they wanted to feature my EP in their "Indie Spotlight" category. KCRW played my song on their station, which is how Josh Radnor discovered me, and subsequently, "Sea Green, See Blue" became the finale song for season two of *How I Met Your Mother*. Later, 14 of my songs would score his award-winning film, *HappyThankYouMorePlease*.

An interesting thing I've discovered is that fans and even film producers don't necessarily care whether a song has been through post-production. In fact, most of the songs I've produced were recorded on my laptop without an external mic. The music was created simply by pressing the record button on Garage Band.

3. How did you grow your audience and keep them updated?

There was a buzz about me in the songwriting scene. At one point, I was even considered the darling of the anti-folk scene. Sometimes, I'd do a residency showcase, which is when you perform at the same venue once a week for an entire month. This is compelling for fans who anticipate a dynamic setlist each week. I would pass around a mailing list and input the names in YMLP, which is still the server I use to send email blasts.

My manager at the time would print flyers to advertise my upcoming shows, and local papers, such as *AM New York* – the one handed out for free as you enter the subway – wrote about me. My music was also shared on popular blog sites.

4. You also had a record deal at some point; how did that happen and how did you end up as an independent artist?

"Sea Green, See Blue" got in the hands of Heavenly Recordings and they released my first official record, *Autumn Fallin'*. I didn't have much presence in the UK/Europe and thought it would be fun to explore new territory. It also provided funding to work with my brother who left his job to manage me. My brother and I moved to London and we toured for 15 months. In 2008, I signed a deal with Blue Note.

About a year later, I was dropped by EMI who owned both labels. Why was I dropped? Probably because I wasn't selling enough records.

Once again, I was Jaymay Music and have been ever since.

5. What are your different income streams?

Hands down, most of my money comes from licensing and often, people will contact me directly with sync opportunities. I also work with a music placement company called Hidden Track Music. My royalties are collected worldwide with a performing rights organization called SESAC. Tunecore collects money from iTunes, Amazon Music, Spotify, and Google Play, and my Bandcamp income is collected through PayPal.

6. How does it work for you with live concerts?

I toured nonstop when I had a record deal, but these days, I don't perform much at all. I have Crohn's disease and touring can be too exhausting for my body. In fact, in April 2013, I had to cancel a major headline tour during my third performance when my body just quit. I couldn't even walk. I had known about my disease for some time, but it never manifested to such an extreme extent. I had to reconsider everything in my life. I moved in with my parents for about a year and drastically changed my diet, perspective, everything.

During that time, I wasn't physically able to make music, so I started an Instagram account, @JaymayMusic. I began posting the paintings

GIVE TO PEOPLE BEFORE
YOU ASK THEM TO GIVE
BACK TO YOU.

and drawings I made from my bed each day. My illness taught me that people have a strong interest in my art as well as my music.

What it really taught me is that your disadvantages are just your tools. You should always ask yourself, "How can I make *this* work for me?"

> **"YOUR DISADVANTAGES ARE YOUR TOOLS. DON'T PITY YOURSELF. INSTEAD, THINK ABOUT HOW YOU CAN MAKE THEM WORK TO YOUR ADVANTAGE!"**

Fans from all around the world continue to purchase my work, and my designs have sold as fine prints to clients such as Oscar de la Renta, Calvin Klein, and Vera Wang. I intend for jaymayart.com to be a major source of income in 2016 and beyond.

7. What does your creative process look like?

When I was 18, I would always write lyrics first and then set them to a melody. Now, my process is more organic and I just spew a load of nonsense until it begins to take shape. Songs can come all at once in a flood where you're merely a vessel and fear claiming the tune as your own. "To Tell The Truth" is a good example of that. Other times, writing can be a painstaking process. "Enlighten Me" took years!

In general, I wake up and do my thing, meaning, I wake up, drink coffee, and sing or draw for three hours in a leopard print bathrobe. I take long walks. I truly stare at the ceiling and think for long stretches of time. For someone who loves music, I spend an awful lot of time in silence. I don't have a strict routine or calendar. If I feel the need to travel, I hop on a train or book a flight abroad (if I can afford it). A new environment can be a great source for inspiration.

I believe in output, output, output. Keep going. Keep doing. Keep creating. Don't worry about failing. "Embrace your ugly" is the best advice I've ever heard. I've learned to not be so pretentious. Deadlines are goldmines. I've learned I work better with a partner or producer who enables me to let things go. I've also learned my work doesn't have to be perfect, or rather, I've accepted that it isn't going to be perfect.

Your work can be raw. When I put something out there, I don't expect people to respond tomorrow. Let time be a judge. Experiment and evolve. People might respond to your work years and years later. Take Facebook, for example, my song they used for their 2013 Mother's Day ad was recorded live with a band back in 2005.

"PRODUCE ART, SHARE IT WITH OTHERS."

8. What's something you would recommend to someone who would like to make an income as a musician?

First, be aware that you have to be incredibly self-motivated. You have to wake up each morning and know you are doing this because you have no other option. If you're willing to fail at what you love, then independence is the right path for you.

My advice to anyone who hates his or her job is simple: quit. Not having a job will force you to find one you desire. It's not okay to not love what you do.

9. What are the greatest challenges for someone who wants to become a professional musician?

Money. What else is new?

The good news is since so many people are streaming music for free these days, they are simultaneously seeking opportunities to directly support the artists they love. Bandcamp, Patreon, and Kickstarter have proven tremendous resources for artist funding.

10. What are some of the resources you would recommend to someone who wants to go into music?

Use social media. It's crucial to have an online presence. Be savvy on the internet; run your website yourself and respond to your fans yourself. Stay present. If you want to be discovered, make it so.

As an independent artist, you have the luxury of growing a career on your own terms. While you may not have the biggest following, the fans you do have are committed to your evolution. They're along for the ride and that's an invaluable investment. Always honor that.

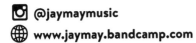

@jaymaymusic
www.jaymay.bandcamp.com

AUTOMATE AND OUTSOURCE

As we approach the end of this book, it's time to highlight some of the other benefits that come with living in the era of digitalization that allow you to have more creative freedom to pursue your passions: automation and outsourcing.

When your business grows, it's an opportunity to find (hopefully!) the right tools and people to help you with tasks that will make the results of your efforts even better!

There are various tools to assist us in giving people what they're looking for when they need it most, and others that help us make the most out of our time on this planet. That's also why I was so keen on having Patty talk to me about her work processes because she's always impressed me with her sassiness of how she navigates the internet.

Whatever it is you have to do repeatedly can probably be automated. The tasks you'd like to find time for but can't should be the tasks in which you look for an automated solution. If you don't find a solution to your problems in the apps, Patty suggests you invest a couple of hours this one time to research how to solve your problem or delegate the task to someone else.

If you're skeptical about automating some of your tasks, you need to consider another perspective. In the earlier days, when people shopped on the street, there were designated times for when you could be there for them and impress them with your kindness. Now, with the internet, everything is available 24/7, and so should the positive experience that comes from your services and/or goods. Whether it's a follow up email that comes immediately after someone trusts you enough to leave their contact information with you to receive your newsletter, or when they buy a product from you, you should always find a way to say thank you.

It might also be that in order for you to provide people with the best possible experience, you might need a number of ideas coming from your community, and thus, you can send them a survey, which is something that can also be automated. Whatever it is you need to serve your clients, customers, and community better should be done in the most efficient way so you can pour all of your energy into serving them.

To make the most out of your most precious resources, your excitement, and your energy, you should outsource the tasks that don't need to be done by you, or those that get to be redundant. For example, when I was a student, I loved receiving requests to accomplish simple tasks because they helped me pay my tuition. Many students use online platforms to offer their help with repetitive tasks. It's people like this who are there to take a load off your shoulders that you don't need to have!

You might think everything's best if you do it yourself, but trust me, it's often the other way around; more eyes usually lead to better results. Also, you can save an immense amount of time if you find someone to help you finish off your work.

People always ask me how I manage to get *so much* done. Sure, I'm self-motivated, but that's hardly the reason for how I accomplish the workload I do.

The truth is, I never finish anything. At least, not by myself. You've probably heard the saying "Done is better than perfect" many times. I'm not really sure how I feel about it because I do prefer to deliver work I consider is as close to perfection as possible, but I don't think I'm someone who can deliver perfection all by myself. Instead, I believe in the 80/20 rule.

The 80/20 rule goes like this: it takes 20% of the overall time to get a task 80% done. Then, it takes 80% of the time to get the last 20% done to make the task perfect. Now, if you outsource the last 20% to someone you trust and expect them to deliver 80% to then finish off their last 20%,

WORK SMARTER,
NOT HARDER!

you'll accomplish what comes very close to perfection without the time investment you'd need if you tried to do it all by yourself.

If you identify where you start slowing down in your work process, it'll be much easier to find someone to work with you. To me, that person is my lovely editor, Diana; at least most of the time, she's the one who makes sure I don't rewrite every single sentence thousands of times. I really wish you find someone as incredible as her.

But then, of course, there are also tasks that don't demand someone as skilled as Diana. You don't need an expert to sort your receipts or research names of people who might be interested in your work! These kind of tasks should, however, also be outsourced to someone who can do them better than you while you do what you do best instead; it's one of the many learnings we creatives need to learn from entrepreneurs and implement in our lives.

Write down tasks you keep procrastinating that take more time than you're okay with spending and look for solutions that won't give you a headache. Okay, I don't want to keep you waiting for Patty's story any longer. She's the expert when I think of automating and outsourcing tasks, so I'll just let her do the talking...

Patty Golsteijn

Meet Patty, an online coach. She created the course Minimal Switch to help self-employed professionals get rid of unnecessary "crap." She provides tips and strategies for people to organize their lives and make their businesses run smoothly.

In her interview, Patty explains why you shouldn't charge per hour, but rather focus on the value you give. Patty also shares her favorite tools to help you become more efficient and manage your workload faster.

📍 **Rotterdam, Netherlands**

1. What's your educational background and how did you arrive to where you are now?

First, when I graduated from high school, I studied applied psychology for one year because I didn't know what I wanted to do yet. It was an orientation year. After that, even though I still didn't know what I wanted to study, I proceeded with media and entertainment management. In my third year, an opportunity came up that enabled me to work and study. I was meant to work for four days and attend classes once a week. However, I loved working and studying just didn't feel appealing to me anymore. I did graduate eventually!

I started working as a project and event manager in one of the university departments and stayed there for two years. It was a slightly chaotic environment and when they couldn't figure out who would become my manager for the following year, I decided to move on and work for myself.

I didn't have any clients or any projects, but I knew I wanted to work for myself, so that's what I did!

I started attending networking events and talked to people about my plans. I made sure people knew where to find me and what I was capable of so when they needed someone, they could reach out to me.

> **"MAKE SURE PEOPLE KNOW WHERE TO FIND YOU AND WHAT TO HIRE YOU FOR."**

I started working on a lot of projects simultaneously; mostly events and projects where I was responsible for the planning and organization. Wearing a lot of hats and getting involved in many projects teaches you to become systematic and highly efficient. I learned to use various online tools to minimize the time I needed to accomplish certain tasks, and I figured I could do something with that knowledge.

I started a company called Regelhelden, which stands for Organizing Heroes. I never liked the term "virtual assistant." To me, an assistant is someone people take for granted and I wanted to change the vibe of the job and give it more meaning. Regelhelden, in my definition, are people who look further than just at the task given to them.

I used to set up workflows for people and I taught them how they could accomplish more in way less time. I basically trained my clients and I also trained the virtual assistants who worked with and for me.

I've always been selective with who I partnered with. I wanted to work with people who were very open-minded and willing to learn new things because I trained people to become more efficient. From my experience, many people just give all their crap to their virtual assistant and expect them to accomplish tasks perfectly. However, people often forget a lot can go wrong if you don't communicate properly. A lot of people get frustrated and the reason for that is usually because of miscommunication.

I didn't say to my clients I was training them, or not explicitly! I think you can train people by asking them the right questions and giving constructive feedback. I would ask my clients to repeat what they said and I would send a follow up email after every conversation to map out the actions we agreed on and how we'll execute them so everything's clear and transparent. Whenever you don't write things down, a lot can go wrong.

"ALWAYS SEND A FOLLOW UP EMAIL."

Another problem of the industry is that clients often expect virtual assistants to deal with their stuff last minute. They send something at 10pm and expect to get it back by 9am the following morning. Unless the virtual assistant is in a different time zone, this behavior just isn't okay.

While running Regelhelden, I learned I didn't want to be the person who does things for others. I wanted to teach people. To me, showing people how they could optimize their processes has a much higher impact than if I would just do everything for them. I want to see my clients succeed by helping them cut out all the unnecessary crap. The idea for Minimal Switch slowly arose.

After a four-day silent retreat, I decided to pivot and only focus on Minimal Switch. When I returned home, even though it was just a four-day escape, I felt incredibly relaxed and knew I wanted to feel like that every day. Before, I was very tense; I'd always sit up and pull up my shoulders. When I then came home, I was able to sit back, which was a very new experience for me. I couldn't stop thinking about what it was, so I scheduled a focus week; a week in complete solitude without social media to think about what I wanted to do with my life. I locked myself in with a big white wall covered in sheets of paper for me to draw and scribble on. My idea was to write everything down that made up my life and start making choices and cut down projects, possessions, and all the things I no longer considered necessary. That's when I decided to focus on helping people find their way to minimalism.

I'm someone who, at all times, does too many things. It's hard for me to pinpoint what I love doing specifically because I get excited about many different things. Nevertheless, I'm very much in touch with my gut feelings so I know when I don't like something, whether it's the people that don't quite fit or the type of project I'm responsible for. I learned to pay more attention to myself. At some point, while working on 15 projects simultaneously, I figured something had to change. Also, I couldn't imagine I was the only person with that sort of problem.

To keep it short, I used to have an agency for personal assistants, but I quit that in 2013 to focus on teaching people how to be more organized and have a content life.

2. How did you pivot your business?

It was a result of the focus week. I launched a simple product page where I wrote, "Do you feel overwhelmed? Would you like to get some peace of mind?" and then I said what I offered. I charged €79. Once people started signing up, I knew I had to do something and actually develop a course.

There was no real launch, no party. From today's perspective, I'd say you should celebrate the launch of a project or a new business not just for yourself, but also for your ambassadors to give them something to talk about. Minimal Switch started with a simple product page. Many people create something and launch it once it's done, and then when no one signs up, they've done all that work for nothing. To me, it makes so much more sense to first get some customers and only then develop a product. You can use Squarespace or Launchrock to create a simple page.

When I changed the direction of my business, it didn't necessarily feel like a pivot because I started blogging about minimalism in 2010. I was trying to get rid of a lot of possessions, which I gradually expanded from just physical possessions to all sorts of stuff in my life; whether it was projects, a particular field of work, or digital overconsumption. I had the content, but just never exploited what I had to its full potential. It was just one of many things I was working on.

I wanted the virtual assistant business to truly flourish, but I also wanted my minimalism classes to expand. I decided to cut everything else I was doing and only focus on these two pillars of my business. However, I slowly realized that in my virtual assistant business, it was me doing things for other people, even though my desire was to teach them to become better. That's how I decided to discontinue the virtual assistant business.

Sometimes, I would love to do more projects, different projects, but then I wouldn't be able to focus on minimalism as much as I want to.

3. What are your different income streams?

I have different products that I sell. I have the Cut the Crap program, which used to be a six week program, then ten, and now it's a 13 week program. When I first launched the course, it was €79, but now it's at €999. I also have a one-on-one program, which runs for three months. When I first launched the program, I charged €299, but now I ask for €1,499. I changed my pricing because I've learned how much value people gain from working with me. I've also published an after-care program called After Patty Kicks for the people who have worked with me to slowly offboard them. And I published books; I'm currently working on the next one.

In the beginning, I just wanted to get a lot of people to participate in my course. After many of them participated, they'd tell me €79 was hardly enough for the work I put into it and for the value they've gained. When you have your customers telling you that you should charge more, you know you're definitely not charging enough! But of course, with pricing, you must know your value and that people truly benefit from your work; otherwise, you'll never have the guts to charge people properly. You'll undervalue yourself!

My pricing is fixed, but if you have custom prices and people say yes immediately, you must charge more! When people say, "Let's do it!" right off the bat, I know I need to ask for more next time. When you feel slightly uncomfortable about asking for that amount of money, you know you've landed at the right amount!

4. How did you build your different programs and income streams?

When I first started, I had the Cut the Crap program and I kept expanding it because I had so much more to say. I wanted to add more value to the people who trusted me and bought my course. One day, someone sent me an email and said that while they enjoyed my course, they wanted to work with me directly. They asked whether I had a one-on-one option and I just said "Yes" and decided to charge them €299 for three months. I didn't have any program, but I developed it while I worked with them via Skype. We scheduled weekly meetings and we talked for an hour. I noticed an hour was too long, so I decided to have 20 minute Skype calls instead. It makes more sense to me to discuss things briefly and encourage action and then follow up.

I really liked the one-on-one sessions with them and decided to do it more frequently. I just had to figure out a system that wouldn't cost too much time. Given the basics were always the same, I started to automate parts of the process. I found tools I thought were valuable and implemented them to keep my workflow as simple as possible.

I use Mailchimp to send automated emails and I use Wufoo, which is my absolute favorite, for surveys that I can embed into my website. My customers answer questions and then I can export a report of their weekly or monthly progress. I also use Google Docs to get answers before every Skype call. The questions are always the same for everyone, which is okay because the content will always be different, but the framework needs to be systematic.

Once people finished working with me, they'd ask whether I had my articles in book form. They wanted a collection because it was more convenient, so I decided to turn my articles into an e-book. There were three main subjects: *Cut the Crap in Your Home, Cut the Crap in Your Life* and *Cut the Crap in Your Work.* That's way too much for just one book, which is why I decided to make a series of three. I sell a bundle of all three books on my website. My customers receive the first book immediately, but the other two books will only be delivered to them once I have finalized them.

I also have the after-care program, which I developed because people wanted to work with me for longer, but I didn't want to be stuck with the same clients forever. I wanted my clients to evolve without me having to hold their hands infinitely. I thought about a good way to slowly offboard them for about a year and a half. I've developed a six month after-care program to help my clients grow while cutting all the crap they don't need from their lives. With every new product I've launched, I've extended the customer lifetime, which has not only helped my clients, but has also helped grow my business.

5. How did you go from running an offline business to setting up an online business?

When you're setting up your own business, you need to listen to yourself and think about what's important to you. You need to make choices that suit you because if you're happy, you'll be better at serving your clients. I once had an appointment with one of my clients who wanted to meet me at their office. I went there and sat next to them and suddenly they got up and left for an appointment. I thought I came to talk about our project, but they wanted me to sit there and act like an employee. Once they came back, they asked if I finished everything. I explained to them that I'm self-employed and I don't trade my time for money. I offer my services to help solve problems. I wanted to choose where I would work and who I would sit next to; being free regarding your choices is the main reason I wanted to work for myself. I knew I had to build an online business.

I believe marketing your business is about building genuine relationships with people. It's simple, but you can't expect immediate results because if you do, you're only set up for the short-term. If you only think in the short-term, you're not building a company, but just selling products. I believe marketing is everything I do. It's every email I send, every conversation I have, every event I decide to attend. Everywhere I go, I market myself and my services. That's part of being a solopreneur. Sometimes, the people you talk to won't become your clients, but they might become your ambassadors and recommend your services to others who need something you offer. And maybe that's an even better way to look at things because if you have ambassadors, the word will spread much faster.

> "EVERYTHING YOU DO, WHETHER IT'S SENDING EMAILS OR ATTENDING EVENTS, IS PART OF MARKETING YOUR SERVICES."

I believe if you're a solopreneur, people who work with you need to trust you, and you need to trust them. Otherwise, the collaboration isn't going to work.

6. What do you outsource or automate and what do you do yourself?

I do all the talking myself and I try to automate everything else. My customers first receive assignments, and then weekly or monthly reviews. The assignments are automated; I use MailChimp for that. I ask for drawings and brainstormings and I ask my clients to scan and send them to me. That's the base for our first Skype call. What comes next are the weekly and monthly reviews, which are pulled into a Wufoo report. I get the filled out forms and sometimes, I respond directly if I see the need. The Skype sessions are usually 20 minutes long and people can schedule the calls themselves. I use Calendly for that. I mark the hours where I want to work and people can schedule their slots themselves.

7. How do you grow your clientele?

I give away a lot for free. People can sign up to my challenges for free, which got me 1,000 people on my mailing list. I also collaborate with others. I once did a webinar series with five other women and because

PEOPLE WHO FEEL A
CONNECTION WITH YOU
ARE YOUR BEST
CUSTOMERS.

we shared our audiences and gave one another exposure, my mailing list grew by 1,400 new subscribers.

When I first started, minimalism was a popular topic and many journalists were interested in talking to me. My work got a lot of attention from the media and I also wrote posts for other blogs. I basically provided others with free content in exchange for a bit of exposure and the possibility to grow my own brand. I also gave talks whenever someone asked me to. I'm always considering the simplest thing I can do that will have the biggest impact, but sometimes you just don't know if something will have a big impact or one at all. Sometimes, you just have to risk it!

"WHAT'S THE SIMPLEST THING THAT HAS THE BIGGEST IMPACT?"

8. What's something you would recommend to someone who wants to go into life coaching?
Automate! Too many consultants want to provide every customer with a custom-made experience, but it's better for your sanity if you build a system and a strategy and then adapt.

As a life coach, you probably have the same set of basic questions for every single client, so why not automate these to be able to focus on the more important things? Your clients will all start at a different stage and they will have different goals and different issues to investigate, so you should really figure out a systematic process and then just allow the content to be different.

9. What are the biggest challenges for someone who wants to become a life coach?
Getting the right type of clients! Not just any clients, but people you genuinely want to work with. It's easiest if you work with people who are just like you, but you're two or three steps ahead of them. I personally believe I have ADD because it's absolutely impossible for me to focus. I get distracted a lot and overwhelmed easily. I'm on my path to figuring it out, so I believe I can help people who struggle the same way I do.

A lot of freelancers who start out think they need to define the right target group, but I believe that's fairly simple because it should be people you can identify with. Look in the mirror. People you can associate with are your clients and people who feel a connection to you are your best customers.

Whatever occupies your mind, and is also constantly present in your life, will be an interesting project for you for the rest of your life. You'll run into challenges every day and then you'll learn how to solve them, making yourself able to help others too.

10. What resources can you recommend to someone who wants to become a life coach?

There are so many great tools; Remember the Milk and Braintoss for to-do lists, StayFocusd and Anti-Social to block out social media, f.lux to adjust the color of your screen according to the outside brightness, and AntiRSI to force yourself to take breaks. I use a roadmap to set long-term goals and plan out my year.

I use Squarespace for my website, and I use Scribd to bookmark all the articles I'm featured in. Mailchimp is my go-to app for email marketing.

Shopify is great as an easy payment method for my e-courses. Then, I use Pathwright to navigate the attendees of my courses through the registration process. Obviously, there's Skype for one-on-one sessions, and then Calendly for people to schedule their own slots. WebinarJam is great for hosting webinars and I use MuteMyMic for muting the input of my microphone. The plugin Caffeine is great for when you want to keep your screen awake during a webinar. I already mentioned Wufoo for surveying people.

I use Buffer for scheduling social media updates and IFTTT for when I want to automatically redistribute content to another platform.

Help Scout is great for when you want to share your mailbox and work, for example, on customer care because you can assign emails to other team members. You should also look at Unroll.me to unsubscribe from all unnecessary newsletters in just one click.

I would also recommend 1Password for keeping all your information safe and to sign up for Private Internet Access if you want to work on-the-go, but simultaneously protect your information. I would also recommend using Time Machine or Dropbox to backup all your data. If you're someone who is on-the-go a lot, then I would say you should install Undercover to your computer. Basically, once you see you do something repeatedly, try to find a solution to automate. It will spare you a lot of unnecessary hustle.

@pattygolsteijn
www.pattygolsteijn.com

FIND STRONG PARTNERS

Slight confession: I've already given a little of the learnings in this chapter away in the previous ones by recommending you work with wonderful people to help you accomplish greater results. However, I don't want you to just think about unique, exceptional people to work with on self-initiated projects. I want you to think about the sort of organizations and representatives that can help you grow and stabilize your solopreneur business. So I didn't give it *all* away...

In more and more cases, companies no longer have an in-house creative team, or at least, not a team that's big enough to accommodate all of the creative work needed. Instead, companies work with freelancers who supply them with fresh ideas and concepts for them to keep up with the latest trends.

Generally speaking, there's a growing number of companies that focus on facilitating peer-to-peer business, such as Etsy, Airbnb, or Creative Market. There are other, more traditional companies that commission you for your creations, which they then sell to their customers. When you make use of peer-to-peer focused platforms, you'll have to deal with the distribution yourself, however, you'll be able to add some personal touch to every package and email you send to your customers. If you manage to find a suitable partner that commissions you merely for your ideas and your digital files, you won't have to deal with any of the distribution, but then you won't be able to add any personal notes either.

Many of the people who now commission work to companies have been proactively asked whether they would be interested in partnering up. People will only ever be able to get in touch with you if they see consistency in your work and admire your personal style. The companies that reach out proactively to people usually do so because someone has linked to their accounts, which brings us back to the importance of social networks and connecting to others on and offline. Given that social influencers can bring brands new customers and can help them become widely known, it makes sense for companies to focus on partnering up with people who have a large online following. It saves them money they would otherwise have to spend on advertising.

But just because no one is writing to you, asking whether you would be willing to work with them, doesn't mean they're not interested in working with you at all. You just have to be the one to approach them first and show them a portfolio of creative work they recognize as potentially profitable.

Most of the companies that commission freelancers invite you to get in touch via their website, but you can always approach a company by sending them an email asking if they work with freelancers if you think your style fits theirs. As you will soon read in Helen's interview, the world belongs to those who ask!

And don't forget that once you agree to work with someone, set up a contract to make sure you've clarified all expectations and deliverables.

However, if you don't hear back from a company you've approached, don't feel defeated. It just means they don't have the customer base for whom your style is suited. You're better off with someone else, so keep putting yourself out there!

As you've heard throughout this book, there are different ways to commission your work. You can either settle on a one-off payment, you can ask for a commission, or if you're lucky, you can get both. As Sara already pointed out, it's normal to get a commission of 3-15% of the retail price.

Once you've agreed on closing a licensing deal, remember to include in your contract when you'll deliver, what sort of files and deliverables are expected, what your work is being used for, and when your partner needs to request additional permissions. Clarify when you expect to be paid, how much, and what will happen if one of you decides to step back from the collaboration.

IN BUSINESS, IT'S ABOUT THE PEOPLE INVOLVED. CHOOSE WISELY!

If you feel uncomfortable negotiating rates and contracts, then the one partner you might want to get on board is a professional agent. An agent is typically responsible for showing your work to potential clients. They represent several professionals in one field and have contacts who hire creatives in the industry. Just like with any representative, you want to work with them because they're well-connected, not necessarily just because they have the capacity to represent you.

Agents help you land jobs and negotiate contracts, and they also handle billing and payments with your clients so you can focus all of your energy on creative work. Having an agent doesn't mean you'll get projects constantly or that you'll have to do every project they suggest to you. However, representatives act in your best interest and help grow your business.

Representatives usually charge up to 50% of every assignment they help you get contracted for. Some agents have a flat-rate commission, others have a tiered commission system, and some charge different fees depending on the type of work you do. You only always pay the agent after you've received your remuneration for the job done.

Getting an agent might be essential to relieve you from the restraints of negotiating terms with clients. If the idea of agreeing on a fee makes you panic, it might be worth the commission they charge to spare you an unnecessary headache.

However, it might take years for an agent to express interest in working with you. Some only work with established professionals. This is, where it once again, pays off to focus on growing your online following because agents are far more likely to help you if they see it will pay off for them. Agents seek creatives with marketable work, which is work that's audience-oriented, something we previously discussed.

Whatever you decide to do, working with or without an agent or setting the goal of hiring an agent at some point, it's important to remember that every partner you choose to work with should help you grow your business as much as you should help them grow theirs.

And now, get ready to meet Helen!

Helen Johannessen

Helen is a model and mould maker in the ceramics industry, and is also a dedicated lecturer. Her greatest strengths are her practical way of thinking and her ability to see opportunities and turn ideas into reality. When she meets new people, she'll often think about the potential spark of collaboration. To Helen, people are the greatest resource to build successful businesses!

📍 **London, UK**

1. What's your educational background and how did you arrive to where you are now?

When I was in school taking A levels, I was studying academic subjects; maths, biology, and French, but I couldn't see how these subjects would fit into the life and career I imagined for myself. I was interested in them, yes, but I thought these topics weren't for me to take any further. I enrolled for an evening class in pottery, which was an unusual hobby at that time for my age at 17, and gained work for a portfolio to apply for an Art Foundation. Once completing that, it led me to taking on a four year degree in ceramics at the Middlesex University in North London. These choices might sound a little unconventional, but I'm not great at following the crowd and accepting rules of life.

During my studies, I realized a degree alone won't make me an expert. I identified two things about myself: that I'm quite practical and solution-driven, and that I enjoy the technical side of the industry. I was always trying to help others at university, especially with the technical side of working with ceramics, and I decided I wanted to do some sort of teaching along with becoming more proficient as a model and mould maker. As a model and mould maker, you create the original object or design and then the plaster moulds to reproduce the original object.

At our degree show in 1995, we had guests from the industry visiting to see our projects. I made sure to speak to them because these people had their own practices and I knew that was my opportunity to try and get contacts or a job. I knew someone who had their own ceramic mould making business was there, so I made sure I spoke to him. I told him confidently without being too arrogant (I'd hoped!) that if he ever needed someone to model and mould make for him, I was his person. He called me the following week.

"MAKE IT YOUR BUSINESS TO TALK TO THE PEOPLE FROM YOUR INDUSTRY."

First, he invited me for a trial week, which is a perfectly acceptable thing to do in the industry. I ended up working there for 18 months before I moved on to another role to widen my knowledge of the making industry. Working with him was like an apprenticeship. As well as running the ceramic business, he also taught part-time at Buckinghamshire University. I used to say to him that, whenever he wanted to quit, I'd be happy to be considered to take over his position. I believe you need to tell people what you want to achieve and make it easy for them to help you reach those goals.

"TELL PEOPLE WHAT YOU WANT TO ACHIEVE. MAKE IT EASY FOR THEM TO HELP YOU REACH YOUR GOALS!"

I then joined a model making and sculpting team in the film industry. I wanted to strategically build my skill set, learn more about the different angles of the maker industry, and use different materials and strategies.

The film industry, at least from my experience, can be highly wasteful, especially back in 1997. It would upset me to see the work we had created to be discarded so quickly after use. We would work long hours per day, weeks, and months on a model, and then after filming the scenes it was made for, the model would invariably be trashed. In the studio where I had worked before, my boss couldn't afford to waste any money on materials. I was earning 30 pounds a day, so I wouldn't waste that amount either. In the film studio, we could use whatever we needed. Often, materials would just get thrown away if it took too long to clean them, so that was not our time well spent.

On one film I worked on, we built a 20th scale model of Trafalgar Square down to the details of all the bus stops, black cabs, trees, sculptures, etc; it was stunning. Most of the scenes using that model were cut out of the movie and it was such a huge model that it had to be discarded. That really had a big impact on me, and I decided it was time for me to move away from that particular industry. I learned a lot and I wanted to get back to a place where people valued other people's work in the way that I appreciated it too.

Things in life usually fall into place, so once I decided to end working there, the seed I had planted in the head of my former boss a while back had flourished; I was invited to Buckinghamshire University to discuss teaching the 3D design course as a visiting lecturer for two days a week. I was 27 at the time, so even though I began lecturing with plenty of relevant experience, I had no formal training for the role. I wanted to evolve as a lecturer and obtain qualifications, so I received a teaching certificate in higher education, which was supported and paid for by the university.

Because of a more regular income, I was able to take the plunge and get myself my first studio space, a basement studio in Finsbury Park. I then started offering my model and mould making services to designers and artists and built a reputation for myself.

Clients came to me with their ideas and I would help them make the tooling or moulds. Sometimes, I would cast a prototype or two, but I wouldn't offer any manufacturing services. I specialized in modeling their concepts and producing moulds.

It was at this time I also started working on my own ideas again. When starting my business, I analyzed my skills and how I could use them to their fullest. I had the urge to translate my creativity into pieces of ceramics. Generally speaking, a good way to approach creativity is to make stuff and explore it to their limits, which sometimes results in "breaking stuff." You can then fix it and learn more for the next project. It's a great attitude to work and live by to be able to cope with uncertainty and then make things work for you.

"MAKE STUFF. BREAK STUFF. THEN FIX IT!"

2. What are your different income streams?

For two decades, I've been model and mould making and have had hundreds of studio clients. I've been lecturing and teaching for the past sixteen years, and I've run my business, Yoyo Ceramics. Over time, it went from building a brand and product ranges, managing production, selling, distribution, and eventually onto licensing my products to other companies.

Client work is not guaranteed regular work. The demand can fluctuate a lot throughout a year. The clients and their needs vary from person to person. When I first started my business, the economy was very different: people were less afraid of taking risks. People were confident in setting up their own product-selling business, they were much happier to invest as the market place was buoyant, and people were spending money. The internet wasn't in full force then as it is now. We've seen a huge rise in competition on pricing and shopping around, so it's a little tougher for the smaller businesses to be seen.

Teaching, for me, has been a major income stream for years. In 2013, I became the Acting Course Leader of a BaHons, so I was much more involved and it needed a lot more of my time and dedication.

Back in 2003, I launched my own brand, Yoyo Ceramics, and to be honest, it wasn't my complete intention, but I wanted to put my work out there and it seemed to fit what I was doing. The first product range was based on mimicking plastic as a material. I designed "Is that Plastic?," which is like a re-work of tupperware and other plastic products, but in brightly-colored glazed ceramic.

My designs gained popularity immediately and I had huge amounts of interest from shops wanting to stock them and press writing features about my work in magazines. I had a few companies quite early on asking me whether I would be willing to license out my work to them.

Licensing was a whole new territory for me. I was hesitant because I only had a small range of products, and if I allowed them to sit under someone else's brand, there was the threat that Yoyo Ceramics wouldn't be able to grow. I turned the offers down because it didn't occur to me I could've just gone back to my studio and produce new designs.

It took about three to four years for me to get the routine in running the business. Selling wholesale, exhibiting at trade shows, and direct selling shows was all new territory for me. It was exciting and had many creative moments, as well as more traditional requirements needed for running your own business. Once I finally felt comfortable being a businesswoman, we had the first recession. The prices of certain things just went crazy. In 2006, the factory that was producing my work in Stoke On Trent closed down because the costs of fuel rocketed. It put a lot of people out of business and suddenly, I didn't have anyone to produce my work, although demand was increasing from the effort I'd been putting in over the years.

I don't know every detail of the economic world, but I think I'm able to recognize patterns. If I see something isn't working in my business for whatever reason, then I won't invest in it further. If I see something's gaining momentum, then that's the aspect I'll focus on.

During the recession, it seemed impossible to find a replacement for my manufacturer, so I went back to some of the people who asked me to license my work to them and asked whether they were still interested. I told them many retailers were interested in selling my work, but I had to turn them away because I had no one to produce my creations. And that's how I started licensing.

For a long time, my income streams were quite balanced. I've only recently started earning more money from teaching compared to the other parts of my business because I became the course leader.

I think it's important that when you juggle a few jobs and have more income streams, you don't do any one thing for three days a week. Once you do something for more than two days a week, I see it as becoming your main job.

Freelancing forces you to think really hard about your work and life balance. At times, it can be challenging to distinguish between weekdays and weekends. Maintain the energy and confidence to know that even if one income stream falls flat, you'll still be able to figure out a different way to make a living. Scheduling holidays and free time can always be the last consideration, but it's really important to give yourself breaks!

3. What does your creative process look like?

That's a very good question. That's where the artist in me emerges; I have many ideas and I sometimes rush to my studio to get them out and into reality. I then keep refining the idea. I worked on my ceramic notepad, for example, for about 18 months on and off. I would just keep reflecting on the design and try to look at it with a fresh pair of eyes again and again, ask friends for feedback and opinions. When I create something new, I generally have no deadline. It's great to be able to work in this way, as I can just keep playing until I'm fully satisfied. I never want to pigeonhole myself and only do homeware, so I grant myself the

CREATE TO FEED
YOUR CURIOSITY.

freedom to experiment. That's probably why I only license designs that I already have instead of designing upon request.

4. How does licensing work in your industry?

It depends on who you are, who they are, what it is you're selling. When I launched my ceramic notepad, I was receiving emails from people inquiring about ordering huge quantities; sometimes as much as 3,000 units. I didn't have a regular supplier to produce that amount, so it felt reasonable to look for a partner who could produce and handle that many units. Also, I didn't see myself as someone who was processing orders and communicating with manufacturers and warehouses. I was happy to hand that over to someone else.

People often think there are two ways of licensing: one where you get a one-off fee for a design you create based on a brief, or you get a percentage from the sales. Personally, I've never received any money upfront because I've always only sold designs I've completed through to production.

With one license deal I made, we found a manufacturer in Asia. Because of the rising production costs in the UK, we had to look for someone abroad, which I was honestly a little uncomfortable with. The contractor would pay for the tooling, buy stock, and keep records of sales to calculate a percentage I would receive quarterly. With licenses, the amount you can receive per unit sold unfortunately doesn't have a "normal rate" – it really varies and can be agreed upon between the two parties.

The money you get would typically only be a very small percentage of the wholesale price or retail price, so you have to work with partners who sell large volumes. Building these additional income streams can really make a business work well if it's successful. Licensing doesn't pay unless the companies you work with sell several thousands of units, and of course, the majority of products don't keep selling year in, year out; demand for new things is part of our consumer world.

In discussing the first license deal, we immediately talked numbers and the company gave me a projection of sales for the first year or two. The ceramic notepad design sold more than 80,000 units over 3-5 years;

generating a million pounds in the UK's creative economy with one object is a great accomplishment and I'm incredibly proud of that.

Every agreement I've signed has included the right for me to buy the product at wholesale or landed cost price to sell them direct or online. The margins are much higher. It's important to review contracts regularly and always make sure the contracts state what you want right from the start, not exclusively what the other party wants. Many people receive contracts and think they have to accept all the terms. Don't forget that contracts can work in your favor too! If you get a contract handed to you and you don't understand what it says, ask someone who does. Negotiate as much as you need to get the contract that's right for you, a contract you feel confident signing.

It's advisable to work with people or companies that you're happy to be associated with. I launched the ceramic notepad in 2008, and two companies were interested in licensing it. One of them was US-based, and the other one was from the UK. I decided to go with the one in the UK because I liked that they were nearby, and I was able to keep an eye on them, but I didn't associate with their image. It was a collaboration that wasn't the best fit for Yoyo Ceramics. At some point, just thinking about the license made me cringe. It's a shame if you feel that way about something you've created and spent so much time on.

Trust is another important element whenever choosing business partners and negotiating licenses. At the end of the day, your contract is a piece of paper both of you sign. That piece of paper is important, but you have to be really comfortable working with the other party because in business, it's always about the people involved.

I've worked with companies that went bankrupt, and I lost a lot of money. They kept taking on new designers and employees, but didn't pay properly or on time. Eventually, that business went under without a lot of us seeing what was owed. Choose who you work with wisely.

5. How does it work with direct selling shows in the maker industry?
We have an open studio twice a year. I know, whenever we do an event like that, I'm going to sell a lot because it's the right audience who visits.

I know these shows will cover the rent of my studio for the year. It's important to be a part of a strong community.

Our studio is in Central London. Part of our contract agreement is that we participate in these public trading shows. One show is in the spring and the other one is right before Christmas. During these shows, I can also sell my prototypes; the sort of work that's not really suitable to sell elsewhere, but maybe someone will buy it for a reasonable amount and recoup making costs at the least. Many makers don't dare to sell objects they don't think are "good enough," but I always think if I don't like or need something anymore, someone else might. It's a good way to clear out my shelves and let someone else enjoy a bargain. I don't like to be wasteful.

In all the years I've been in my creative business, I've also learned the majority of what businesses sell happens at the end of the year. The entire year is just preparation work for the Christmas season. It sounds bizarre, but that's the way it is.

6. At what trade shows do you sell your creations?

I like to attend the Design Junction and Tent London as a visitor these days. My license deals mean those companies would show my work and deal with the trade shows, an aspect that suited me. I prefer direct selling shows because I enjoy chatting and selling to my customers. They'll often have excitement in their eyes because they're so delighted about their purchase from me. It's important to gain feedback from their end being the customer. I like that part. I love selling to the people who might come back in a year or two and tell me they still love what they bought from me.

There are a lot of different markets or sales opportunities around London most weekends. Some of the markets are a bit more "craftier" than others. Some are targeted at hobbyists to sell their creations. These market opportunities are great because they gain appreciation of the smaller businesses from the public. They're cheap to exhibit at and usually pay off. In recent years, I've also been gradually relying on online sales, of course.

7. How do you use the internet to market and sell your work?

When I first started Yoyo Ceramics, I didn't have a website. No one did back then because it was expensive to have someone to build a website for a small business, so I had my first website built for me in 2005. My current website needs an update, but when I first commissioned the company to make me this one, what we did was really revolutionary; it linked to all the available social networks that were quite new then. I've always made sure to have high-quality photos for publicity. I uploaded all my product pictures to Flickr and then we would pull these images to my website. Now, that sounds very old fashioned, but back in the day, our approach created a social spiral. It's important to think in loops when you try to make the internet work for you. Now, you might do it the other way around, like host your product pictures on your page and use Pinterest, for example, to share them with others.

Years ago, many of my clients I made moulds for didn't have their own selling website, so I offered to sell the products I created for them on my website and get a commission from the sales. Now, these people have slowly implemented shops into their own websites and there's no longer a need for me to do that. Making decisions and offering services that are right in the moment are important to think about. They're opportunities for everyone.

8. What resources would you recommend to makers?

It depends on where you're based. In the UK, Hidden Art was a great organization to get advice and expertise when I first started Yoyo Ceramics; they really helped me get my business off the ground. The British Library is a great place for startups because they have the Business and IP Center. They connect makers and creatives with mentors and have great resources. There are a lot of creative websites that can be useful too, like The Design Trust, Nesta, The Design Council, and The Crafts Council, which are all worth researching for different aspects of a creative career.

As a maker, you must be proactive and see everyone you meet as a great resource. When I meet someone, I often imagine how we could collaborate. I always see some sort of potential in people I come across, whether it turns into anything or not!

9. What are the greatest challenges for someone who wants to be a professional maker?

I remember the first time a customer came to my studio and walked away with some of my creations. I felt like they had taken my child! I will never forget that. Everything I make feels very personal to me; it contains a bit of my personality. Being a maker means you're giving a piece of yourself to people. You must have a relationship with the products you make, or otherwise, it could become a bit of a dry business and you might lose interest in making.

Another challenge for makers is the need to have a two-sided business; you must make your products available online, but also have a presence where you sell to people directly in the real world. That really helps spread the word about what you do in different ways.

10. What's something you would recommend to someone who wants to become a maker?

Start planting seeds for you to build a business. Talk to people and tell them about your plans. Work hard!

Try not to look at others and figure out what strategy they applied that seemingly worked for them because you can guarantee it didn't work out overnight. Whatever you see that's successful, you can be damn sure they put in lot of work. Many hours have been spent working on their business to create the output you see. You can't build a business if you're not self-motivated, so all the other people whose work you see and admire are really hard, dedicated workers!

@helenyoyo
www.yoyoceramics.co.uk

PLAN YOUR LONG-TERM GOALS

Time to dig deep: How would you like to *feel* every day when you wake up in the morning? How do you wish to be spending your days? And who would you like to be spending your days with?

Often, when we think about our life goals, we think about our definition of success. Nevertheless, it's a definition that's hardly ever coined by our deepest, personal desires. What's regarded as "successful" has been defined by what our friends, family, and the society we are a part of consider as such.

It's easy to be able to say, "I work for Google." People know and respect the company. There's no need for justification because once you work for a well-known company, you're immediately regarded as someone who has "made it." If you, instead, decide to walk your own path, you'll most likely have to defend your decision many times, especially when things don't go smoothly from the start or get rough every now and then. (Which is normal, but no one ever posts about it on Instagram.)

Because of social media, we're constantly exposed to the successes of other people (who are often younger than us, on top of everything else). It's not easy to say I'm a photographer, an illustrator, or another type of digital creative who's making it every day, but is still far away from having actually "made it." And even if other people consider you as successful and someone who's made it, chances are high that deep down, you still feel like you're making it every single day, which you probably are!

It might come as a surprise to you that people with 200K+ followers are hustling each day and trying to make it too. There's clearly no difference between someone who you think has made it and someone who feels like they're trying to make it.

In school, university, and the jobs we've gotten afterwards, we've always been challenged with goals we've worked towards, and we've been comparing ourselves to the people we're surrounded by. However, once you're self-employed and you've reached the point where you can support yourself with your creative work, you might ask the question, "What's next?"

Given our society aspires to be bigger, better, and richer, you might be wondering what you should work towards next. You might ask whether you should expand your business and build an actual company. But do you really want to be spending your days managing and motivating other people, or do you want to be creating? How do you want to be spending your days? How do you want to feel every day? And where does what you think you want come from? Is it really what you want, or is it what you believe you want?

It might be that you still have a job and picked up this book to learn more about what it takes to not get a monthly paycheck from your employer. In that case, your desire to become independent is what you might define as your goal. But again, are you aware of what it takes to be self-employed? Is it what you really want because you want to spend more time with your family, or do you want to be able to travel the world?

Recently, being a freelancer has been hyped in the media, so it seems like a thing that's "to be desired." Again, consider how you want to feel and how you want to spend your days. As creative freelancer, you'll only be spending about half of your time creating and the rest of your time doing a lot of things entire teams split responsibilities to complete when working for a company. There's no project manager to prepare a detailed brief for you; no one else to deal with the nitty gritty stuff. Is this what you want?

It's important to think about the questions I've posed in this chapter and write down your conclusions. You can't and shouldn't compare yourself to other people. Take the time to sit down and reflect on what you want your process to look like. Then, think about how you want to

MAKE YOUR PROCESS
YOUR EVERYDAY GOAL.

be challenging yourself. Reflect on what steps you'll take to free up your time to focus on exploring what else the world has for you that fits who you are.

Let's go back to the question of what success means to you; is it being recognized by people, or being able to make enough money from drawing, designing, or writing so you can spend time with your family? Once you start comparing yourself to others, you only compare yourself to the impressions available to you because you don't know what sacrifices these people made to get to where they are. You haven't seen them sitting behind their computer at 2am trying to finish something. You've probably only seen a picture of a drink at the pool or how they walk their dog at the beach.

Write down what success means to you and go back to that piece of paper whenever you face a decision you're unsure about. I believe that once you write down how your successful self wants to be spending days, it'll be much easier to feel happy about your life without comparing yourself to others.

That piece of paper will also make it easier to say "No" to great offers that don't bring you closer to how you want to feel in your life. And once you know with whom you want to be spending your days with, it'll be easier to know what to focus your energy on in order to reach just that.

When I first reached out to the women I interviewed for this book, I didn't know some had kids. For them, the determination to build scalable income streams came out of necessity. They have a family they wanted to spend more time with. It was clear to them how they wanted to be spending their days. They defined their everyday journey, not a peak somewhere far away.

Think and write: How do you want to feel when you wake up? How do you want to be spending your days? And what can you do to reach that? Now, it's time for the last story. I'm pleased to introduce you to Lisa!

Lisa Glanz

Lisa is an illustrator who specializes in creating assets for graphic designers. She knows what designers need in their day-to-day because she was one herself. Lisa speaks about the importance of remembering where you came from and knowing where you're heading in your professional life. To her, once you know how you want to feel in your day-to-day, you'll be much more focused on reaching it.

In her interview, Lisa explains how to master the internet: you just have to know what you're searching for.

📍 **Cape Town, South Africa**

1. What's your educational background and how did you arrive to where you are now?

I studied advertising and graphic design. I wished to become an illustrator, but there weren't many job opportunities because it wasn't considered a "proper job" back then. Graphic design was the next best thing. I must say I really enjoyed the layout and typography aspect to the job, so I was happy with my choice in the end. After graduation, I decided to get a job in the magazine industry instead of advertising. Advertising usually attracts a certain type of person and I wasn't quite one of them. I managed to move up the corporate ladder and after about six years, I became an art director. However, I knew I didn't want to be doing this forever; I knew I wanted more from my career.

The older I got, the more I learned about who I was and what I wanted to do with my life. I decided to quit. I had a friend who had her own graphic design studio and she offered me a unique opportunity. We had an agreement that I would spend the mornings working on her projects and then in the afternoon, I worked on my own. I had access to all her equipment and in return, I paid her a portion of my earnings. After about two years, my business grew so much that I couldn't sustain working for her half-day. We ended up parting ways and I moved into my own studio in the city before I moved my studio into our home.

I had space there, especially mental space, to think. The energy of the house boosted my creativity, so I started experimenting and trying out new things. My desire to become an illustrator never stopped nagging me, so I started illustrating again.

At the beginning of 2015, I was able to discontinue my graphic design studio to focus on illustration instead. Even though I pivoted my business entirely, 2015 was my best year. It's probably also because I quit my graphic design business only once I was earning more with my illustrations. During the transition, I was working about 60 hours a week. I still work most days including the weekend, but it's now about 48-50 hours.

2. What are your different income streams?

I have an Etsy store and a shop on Creative Market, which makes for the majority of my income. I also participate in Bundle Deals on

DesignCuts.com every three months or so. On both markets, Etsy and Creative Market, I sell digital resources. There's no shipping involved. Although the products are the same, the two markets are different because they serve different target groups.

On Etsy, many of my customers are scrapbookers and end-consumers who use my products for fun. Creative Market, on the other hand, caters mainly to graphic designers. Their audience uses Creative Market for professional purposes. I would say my graphic design background helps with understanding the buyer's needs. The inside knowledge of knowing what graphic designers are looking for is a great advantage, so I create graphic sets I think will be useful to them and bundle them based on various themes. I also have a following of photographers who buy my work. They usually use my illustrations to overlay their photos.

And then, the bundle deals are something I've been experimenting with because they've been generating a significant part of my income. DesignCuts bundles graphic design resources and sells them to graphic designers at a discounted price.

I'm now earning dollars instead of South African rands. That's boosted my income, and it's probably why I could discontinue my graphic design business so quickly. I'm not sure if an American illustrator could live off my earnings, but given the dollar/rand exchange at the moment, as a South African, online market spaces aren't just a great way to make my work visible to everyone around the world, but it gives me enough of an income to have a good life.

3. How and why did you launch your different businesses?

In South Africa, we often feel very removed from the rest of the world. Many of us feel like we're living on an island. We rely heavily on the internet to learn about new trends and what other people are up to.

I'm generally very interested and inspired by what other creatives do, which is why I research a lot. One day, I was looking through Etsy and I found a store that only sold digital assets. They've done an incredible amount of sales, close to 150,000, so I looked through what they offered and it nudged me that if they could do it, I could do it too!

Once my Etsy store was up, I started looking for other outlets where I could sell my work and I came across Creative Market. I applied to open a store there and after a quick screening, I was in. They review your portfolio and if your work is up to their standards, you'll get access as a seller. Retrospectively, opening a store on Creative Market changed my entire life because I can now illustrate for a living.

Whenever you join a new market space, you first need to analyze its community. I would recommend looking at the most successful people every time you decide to get involved with a new platform. With Creative Market, it's easy to spot who the leaders are because the products are ranked based on their earnings and popularity. The products you see first are the ones earning the most with the highest number of sales.

When you look at the community leaders, try to understand what they do that makes them successful. How do they present their work? How do they talk about their work? What type of products work best for them? I'm not saying you should copy them (it's important to develop your own style and signature products), but I think you can learn from them in terms of what makes a great product, what makes a digital store successful, and what the community demands are in each market.

With DesignCuts, it was easy. They approached me and I was curious if this would be something that could work for me, so I just figured I should try. I get a lot of requests from various sites, but I stick to DesignCuts because I don't want to sell out. I prefer to focus on quality work instead of budget deals. I don't want to harm my brand.

4. How do you decide what to work on next?

I believe it's a combination of instinct mixed with what you see is already doing well. On one hand, I focus on creating assets that are inspired by various holidays and seasons, such as Easter, Christmas, or Mother's Day, but on the other hand, I look at things that are trending and produce something with my own twist. Ideas come to me while I'm out for a run or walking my dog. Sometimes, I try out ideas not knowing if they'll work or not. That's what makes this process so much fun; there's so much room for experimentation and you're never 100% sure what will work out.

I'm trying to produce at least one product a month. Products, by my definition, are graphic illustrations and elements bundled together for graphic designers to use in their work. My products range from about 65 to 450 elements per bundle consisting of anything from a watercolor flower to a pre-made logo design. The price range varies based on the amount of elements within the product. If you produce a smaller bundle, you generally can't ask for the same amount of money you would for a 450 element bundle. You don't want to over-price your products to remain competitive; you need to find a balance. Cheaper bundles will sell more, but you need to sell a lot of them to earn enough income so you can remain creative.

5. What's the goal of your business?

Before I dared to try myself out as a freelance illustrator, I read a lot of self-help books. One of them suggested asking yourself how you wanted to feel every day. Usually, people ask you what you want to do and what you want to achieve, but no one ever asks you how you want to *feel*.

How do you want to feel when you wake up in the morning? What kind of life do you want to have? What should your day consist of?

I knew I wanted to be independent. I knew I wanted to earn dollars to boost my income, and I knew I wanted to feel vital and energetic, which was how I felt whenever I was illustrating. Once I could recognize what I wanted, I became extremely focused.

When you're self-employed, you learn many important life skills because you're not only figuring out how to make a living, but you're also constantly refining who you are as a person and what goals you pursue. And because you're in charge, your decisions and choices define your values.

Many of my friends say I'm lucky because I can walk my dog on the beach every day and I work from home with no rigid hours, but I can only reply that I work to be where I am. I sacrificed a lot to get to where I am with my business and my life. It really depends on how badly you want something. If your goal is everything to you, nothing's going to stop you.

With creativity, the goal should be all about the creative process and not necessarily the outcome. It's easier said than done, and as we often focus on the results, it's only natural. But I believe it's about how you want to feel every day while you're in the process of living and the energy you put in to produce and market your work to make an income. There won't be a peak, at least not one that's clearly defined for you. You won't move up the corporate ladder. Instead, you'll become more skilled at what you do if you do it every day. Your process will become your everyday goal and how you'll achieve your dreams. My ambition is to eventually be a recognized surface pattern designer and illustrator. I want to be approached to do editorial and licensing work, but I know it takes time to get there.

6. What do you do to grow your business?

I've learned that half of selling your work online is all about how you present it. You can have the most gorgeous product, but if it's not presented properly, no one is going to care. First impressions are everything!

I've also learned I need to spend time creating preview slides to show my customers specifically how they could use the elements in their work. Giving them as many details as possible about the product before they're prompted to purchase is important.

"FIRST IMPRESSIONS ARE EVERYTHING!"

Your layout, what colors you use; it all really matters. If your cover slide doesn't look great, people aren't going to click through to your product. Always check whether your description is easy to read and feels inviting. I'd even say if you want to open a digital store, presentation alone is 50% of your product. Budget the time and don't be impetuous.

To grow my business, I also started using Pinterest to get traffic to my stores. Besides that, I'm on Behance and I use Instagram to share snapshots of my work in progress. I already got commissioned for work because someone found me on Behance. If you want to make money as an illustrator or a graphic designer, you need to be involved in relevant communities.

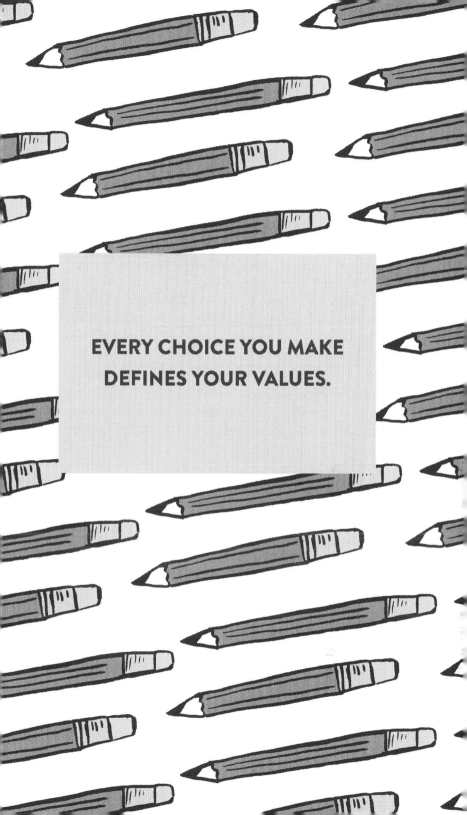

7. How do you improve the customer experience over time?

My goal, with whatever I do, is to give my customers more than they expected. I'm trying to be authentic at all times. I believe people can relate more to those who are honest and genuine. People sense if you're fake and doing things just for money. I want people to feel great about buying from me!

8. What resources would you like to recommend to someone who wants to start a business such as yours?

There are millions of resources and it always depends on what you're looking for. Whatever platform, whatever community you want to join, that's the one you should spend the most time researching. Every platform is unique and every single one works differently. Take the time and learn more about the community you want to be a part of, especially if you want to make money there.

If you need to find a way to define your goals, I would recommend Marie Forleo's course.

I'm also a member of Skillshare because it gives you the possibility to dive into different subjects; some of them are related to your business, others not as directly. It's a great resource to get fresh insights.

You have to keep improving your skills. I thought I was very professional in my use of Adobe software, but since I started selling digital assets to other designers, I've at least doubled the level of my skills. You can learn anything you want, but you must be willing to do so and Skillshare is a great place to start.

9. What's a piece of advice you would give to someone who wants to start a business such as yours?

Research how your products are being used to understand how people use them as much as you can. For example, my preferred software is Illustrator, so I don't use Photoshop as much. I know that my products are being used in Photoshop, so I started making an effort to learn how people use it in order to serve them better.

10. What are the greatest challenges for someone who wants to start a business such as yours?

Time management is a huge challenge. When you're self-employed, you're not just creating all the time; you're running a business. I spend a lot of time with customer support and while I love receiving emails from people from all around the world, it's also time-consuming. However, customer support is my first priority because I want people to have a great experience when they buy from me so they're happy with their purchase. Figuring out a balance between being there for people who buy my products and having the time to create new ones has been my biggest challenge.

You'll also need to learn to prioritize. You won't be able to work on everything you'd like to, at least not immediately. For next year, I'm planning to sit down at the end of the year for two days and map out my focus for the upcoming year. I'll break the year up month by month, and even week by week, and specify what I want to focus on in the upcoming months. I think it's important to set yourself goals to be able to see where you're heading. Otherwise, you won't know when to celebrate your successes. So if you haven't already, you should make that plan today. For yourself. And for your goals!

@glanzgraphics
www.lisaglanz.com

SAY HELLO!

Thank you for picking up this book and spending your precious time with us. We hope you've collected many ideas while reading this little guide we've created to help you think about how to stabilize your freelance business.

We hope that wherever you are on your freelance venture, whether it's just stepping on the path towards professional independence or looking for an idea to challenge yourself with, we hope this book has given you the needed inspiration and some ideas for how to master it!

We'd be extremely grateful if you'd write an Amazon or a GoodReads review for *My Creative (Side) Business* so we know what we've done right and how we could serve you better when we start working on the next book.

We'd also really appreciate it if you'd get in touch to share with us what this book has inspired you to do. Also, feel free to tell us what other topics you'd like us to explore and write about! We'd simply love if you'd say hello on Twitter, Instagram, or send us an email!

If you've supported us during our Kickstarter campaign, turn a couple of pages; that's where you'll find your name! And if you're curious who supported us and what they do, or if you're looking for someone in your own area of interest, look at those pages because these are the people sitting with us in the same boat. I'm sure they'll appreciate it if you connect with them and ask how they're doing or involve them in a project of yours!

In case you have some more questions you think I might be able to answer, feel free to send me an email to hello@mkanokova.com, and if you just want to get a weekly piece of inspiration and hear what I've learned while trying to make it as a freelancer, then please sign up to my personal newsletter on my website: mkanokova.com.

If you're fascinated by the beautiful artwork in this book, check out Sara's website or her Instagram stream. If you enjoyed the layout and want to know who's responsible for it, look up Diana's work. And if you want to know who the word magician is who made sure the text read well, look up Diana Jean's website.

Thank you for your support and good luck on your path. We know you'll make it.

See you somewhere on the internet!
Love,
Monika, Sara, Diana, and Diana Jean

MONIKA KANOKOVA

Monika Kanokova gave up long ago on trying to define one single location as her home as much as she has given up on trying to find a job title that would summarize what she does. She has a fascination for city building and space design and its impact on people's lives. Her interest in social mobility has planted her interest in people's stories and their unique career paths. She specializes in technology-based communication solutions for them to have positive impact on their relationships.

Legally, she's a freelance advertiser, but as she doesn't believe in classic advertising, her design-driven approach often leads to unconventional solutions.

She helps her clients build useful products, and optimizes customer relationships and communication by adding value to people's lives. If you're wondering how you could improve the communication with your customers or local communities, don't hesitate to contact her.

 www.mkanokova.com
@mkanokova
 **hello@mkanokova.com**

SARA COMBS

Sara Combs is an artist and a designer whose focus is creating intuitive and meaningful experiences. She uses a variety of mediums to do so; everything from UI/UX design for both web and apps, to pattern design and illustration, and interior design for her latest project, The Joshua Tree House (an Airbnb rental in the Mojave desert).

Since moving to California after graduating from the Maryland Institute College of Art, she's been in love with the state's landscape and laid back way of life.

 www.designcomb.com
 @saracombs
 sara@designcomb.com

DIANA JEAN JOINER

Diana J. Joiner is an e-commerce copywriter within the fashion industry, and is also a freelance editor and proofreader, living in a beach town on Maryland's east coast. After graduating with an English degree with a focus in teaching, she went abroad to Southeast Asia where she taught English in Thailand and traveled for seven months. Upon returning to the US, she decided to adjust her career path to pursue writing and editing.

Her debut freelance project was editing *This Year Will Be Different*. Now, she's back again with her second publication as she continues to make her proofreading/editing career flourish on the side. Paying close attention to detail, strategically piecing words together to form beautifully-crafted sentences with depth and impact, and creating consistent fluidity is what she strives to do in every project she's involved in.

Grammar is her passion and her passion is grammar. And music. And the beach. Obviously.

 www.dianajoiner.com
@JoinerEdits
djjoiner925@gmail.com

DIANA OVEZEA

Diana Ovezea is a graphic and type designer, currently based in Amsterdam, who embraces being an "international." She spent her childhood in Romania and most of her school years in Austria. After graduating from the Type and Media master class at the Royal Academy of Arts in The Hague (KABK), she stayed in the Netherlands to pursue type design as a full-time career.

She loves the challenge of complex typographic projects. No matter whether she's working on a new logo, a book, or a large type family, she makes an effort to create structure and meaning in her client's projects. She only has one requirement for a potential client or colleague: passion.

Diana mentors type design workshops in the summer and teaches typography to graphic design students at KABK in the winter.

 www.ovezea.com
 @TypeThoughts
 type.design@me.com

(DRUM ROLL)

...

MEET THE KICKSTARTER BACKERS

...

WHO MADE THIS PROJECT HAPPEN

...

THANK YOU!

...

For the second time, we were successfully funded on Kickstarter! Yay and thank you so much, everyone!

Last year, I received a couple of emails telling me that people who appeared on the list published in *This Year Will Be Different* were hired for a freelance assignment. Because we wanted to keep up the tradition, we asked our wonderful backers for their contact details again. If you're looking for someone to help you realize a project, please reach out to someone from our community.

ANIMATION

Yves Das	BE	loopingtales.com

BRAND STRATEGY

Angela Fürstberger	AT	linkedin.com/in/afuerstberger
Daniela Terbu	AT	coolhunting.at
Sarah Kickinger	AT	ravenandfinch.com
Nik Baerten	BE	pantopicon.be
Melanie Böhme	DE	simel.coffee
Steffen Staeuber	DE	createmeaning.com
Fiona Mandos	GB	letskiss.design
Mark Janson	GB	markjanson.com
Arjen Heus	NL	www.frankycherry.com
Anika Horn	USA	anikahorn.com

COACHING

Ashley Oppon	USA	dreadlocktarot.com
Elaine Watson	USA	readytopause.com
Mary Wissinger	USA	chinupheartopen.com
Suzanne Gochenouer	USA	transformationaleditor.com

COMMUNICATIONS

Alexandra Prasch	AT	contentessa.at
Dominik Berger	AT	dobe-media.eu
Kai Wichmann	AT	wearebetter.at
Klaus Heller	AT	klausheller.at
Lisa Brandstötter	AT	boomcreativelab.com
Lukas Havranek	AT	lukashavranek.com
Martina Loesch	AT	spunkyrella.com
Michaela Schmitz	AT	backofficeandmore.at
Natalie Opocensky	AT	digitalnomadin.at

Sarah Krobath	AT	sattgetextet.com
Susi Mayer	AT	urhaus.net
Franziska Schmid	DE	veggie-love.de
Ina Bohse	DE	peopleonmyway.com
Michael Jones	DE	eyeem.com/michael
Sandra Stabenow	DE	www.frau-frei-und.de
Robbie Dale	GB	robbi.es
Frances Thompson	NL	fmthompson.com
Margot van der Krogt	NL	maeandmany.com
Courtney Balestier	USA	courtneybalestier.com
Elizabeth Wellington	USA	lizwellington.com
Gus McAllibaster	USA	gusmcallibaster.com
Kira Parker	USA	edgedwhimsy.com
Kiri Milburn	USA	makethecuteface.com
Sarah Anderson	USA	spitfirescribe.com
Tasha Turner	USA	tasha-turner.com

CRAFTS

Sophie Pester	DE	supercraftlab.com
Jerolyn Crute Sackman	USA	etsy.com/shop/PaperArboretum

CROWDFUNDING STRATEGY

Cloed Priscilla Baumgartner	AT	priscillaandpat.com
Wolfgang Gumpelmaier	AT	crowdfunding-service.com

DEVELOPMENT

Aaron Cruz	AT	aaroncruz.com
André Kishimoto	BR	kishimotostudios.com
Martyn Haigh	GB	martynhaigh.com
Richard Davey	GB	photonstorm.com

DIGITAL PRODUCT DESIGN

Kristen Gellrich	CA	wildhearteddesign.com
Alfred Nerstu	DK	alfrednerstu.com
Sarper Erel	DK	sarper.se
William Hollowell	SE	hollowell.se
Alexander Rekas	USA	alexrekas.com

EVENT SERVICES

Sophie Holzapfel-Epstein	AT	swarinasweets.at
Tina Hinterleitner	AT	hellbunt-events.at
Patricia Martin	DE	instagram.com/ofenkatze
Rachel Drudi	USA	racheldrudi.com

FASHION

Julia Annamariaangelika Müller	DE	annamariaangelika.de
Veronika Kavkova	GB	kavkajewels.com
Melissa Aho	USA	melissaaho.com
Sharon Rowe	USA	www.ecobags.com

ILLUSTRATION

Fredy Santiago	USA	imsugarcoated.com
Peter L Brown	USA	thetoonist.com
Raven Henderson	USA	artfuldevo.com

Performing Arts

Hendrik Leenders	BE	urbandancefloor.be
Frida Backman	GB	fridabackman.com
Sydney Levinson	GB	barryslounge.co.uk

PHOTOGRAPHY

Ana Sampaio Barros	AT	instagram.com/anasbarros
Elisabeth Bernhofer	AT	elisabeth-bernhofer.at
Kristina Satori	AT	kristinasatori.com
Michèle Pauty	AT	michelepauty.com
Ursula Schmitz	AT	ursulaschmitz.com
Caryn Christie	CA	www.timeinglass.com
Jakob Kjøller	DK	jakobkjoller.com
Eleonora Festari	IT	www.eleonorafestari.it

PRODUCT DESIGN

Johann Kaindlstorfer	AT	industriellegestaltung.at
Mag. Richard Deimel	AT	extravaganzas.at
Talia Radford	AT	taliaystudio.com

RESEARCH

Dr. Volker Göbbels	DE	technologyscout.net
Madoka Suganuma	JP	japancreativeinsights.com

SALES

Sergey Erlikh	NL	www.cloudimpact.biz

STYLING

Sabine Reiter	AT	craft-up.com

VISUAL DESIGN

Anna Aurelia Grubelnig	AT	bueroaurelia.at
Eva Lettner	AT	evalettner.com
Maximilian Huber	AT	wearecellardoor.com
Maximilian Mauracher	AT	maximilianmauracher.com

Nina Ullrich	AT	designnomadin.com
Wolfgang Hartl	AT	amstein.at
Elise Vandeplancke	BE	elisevandeplancke.be
Monica J. Chhugani	CA	www.monieredesigns.com
Jørgen Smidstrup	DE	lowereastlab.de
Stephan Kluwe	DE	creanetivity.com
Hameed Mohammed	GB	winterphoto.co
Sorrel Rivers	GB	sorrel-rivers-art.com
Isabelle Mattern	LU	isabellemattern.com
Lee Jun Lin	SG	leejunlin.com
Amber Kahler	USA	behance.net/amberkahler
Denis P. Castillo Moncada	USA	hellodenis.com
Heath Vaughn Clark	USA	design4mfg.com
Janae Newman	USA	eksteindesign.com
Klangwelt	USA	klangwelt.com
Sarah Barrett	USA	sarahbbarrett.com

The finalization of this book was also supported by Ani Bagdasaryan, Arne Brill, Ben Stinnett, Ben Weavet, Bridget Best, Claas Jäger, Daiga Miezite, Darek Anthony Dumon, Delanghe, Dominik Frixeder, Greg Hoyos, Isabel Firneis, Laurent Mertens, Luca Morassi, Mac Joiner, Mathias Lynders, Maureen Kushmore, Sebastian Elke, Troy Raymond and 330 other incredible people. Thank you!

THANK YOU
TO OUR REVIEWERS

We're grateful *My Creative (Side) Business* was reviewed by people we admire greatly, so we'd love for you to check out their work:

SEAN BLANDA / *editor-in-chief and director at 99U*
Instead of inspiration, 99U provides creatives with pragmatic and actionable advice from leading researchers and visionary creatives to help you build on the ideas you already have. Follow 99U.com for detailed instructions to make ideas happen.

KATY COWAN / *founding editor of Creative Boom and MD at Boomerang PR*
An online magazine that inspires and supports creative professionals worldwide. If you love arts, crafts, graphic design, illustration, and photography, head over to creativeboom.com for tips, resources, and advice to succeed in your business.

PAUL JARVIS / *creator of the Creative Class*
An insightful course and network that teaches everything there is to know about freelancing; from defining a niche, to creating a killer portfolio, to pricing your services. If it sounds like something for you, visit creativeclass.io.

JOHN LEE DUMAS / *founder and host of Entrepreneur on Fire*
A top ranked business podcast with the most inspiring entrepreneurs. You'll learn more about people's biggest failures, their lessons learned, and their turning points of success. Tune in on eofire.com.

KATE KENDALL / *founder and CEO at Cloudpeeps*
A talent marketplace that matches businesses with the world's top freelance marketing, content, and community professionals who align with their mission and create meaningful work. Sounds interesting? Then visit cloudpeeps.com.

GET MY FIRST BOOK!

Thank you for reading my second book to the very end! If you haven't read *This Year Will Be Different: The insightful guide to becoming a freelancer*, you can find it on Amazon. If you've read and loved both books and definitely want to know about the next guide for freelancers, please sign up to this list to get notified once we're ready for taking pre-orders: bit.ly/newpublications

---

Print-on-demand
and Kindle versions
available on Amazon

WRITE A REVIEW AND GET A PRESENT!

... and if you want to share your love, please write us an Amazon review, send us a screenshot and your postal address to hello@mkanokova.com and we'll send you a small present as a thank you.

Printed in Great Britain
by Amazon